Reading Between the Signs

Scripture quotations are from New Revised Standard Version Bible, copyright © 1989 National Council of the Churches of Christ in the United States of America. Used by permission. All rights reserved.

ISBN: 978-1-5051-1228-3

ACS Books is an imprint of TAN Books
PO Box 410487
Charlotte, NC 28241
www.TANBooks.com

Printed and bound in the United States of America.

Reading Between the Signs

Unexpected Directions on the Ultimate Journey

Rhonda Zweber

ACS BOOKS

It is not often that a book grabs you and keeps your heart and soul engaged throughout. Rhonda Zweber has crafted a beautiful testament to her unbending faith through her health challenges using scripture passages linked to storytelling. This book is a journey through many joys and difficult times told with honesty and humility. As a metastatic breast cancer survivor myself, each chapter resonated with my own walk with the Lord and offered pearls of Rhonda's wisdom as well. This book is a "must read" for anyone who has struggled with illness or loss and yearning for a closer walk with the Lord.

DR. SUE ANN GRUVER *Superintendent, Prior Lake-Savage Area Schools (2008-2015)*

With her poignantly positive memoir, *Reading Between the Signs*, Rhonda Zweber provides spiritual wisdom based upon her own journey as a cancer survivor. Rhonda offers unique and engaging reflections on some of the Bible's most important passages, inviting the reader to embrace scripture and a relationship with Jesus Christ in facing their own unique life challenges. Walk with Rhonda as you face your own burdens and realize that when you follow God's signs, you are never alone.

LISA M. HENDEY *Founder, CatholicMom.com* *Author,* The Grace of Yes

---

Theology left on the page is interesting and good for conversation, but when someone takes the truths of the faith and puts them into practice in the midst of a struggle, you have a message. Rhonda has a message for you in the midst of your struggle, whatever it may be. I'm inspired by Rhonda's story of tenacity in the face of overwhelming odds and her faithfulness to Christ in the midst of what the world would call "uncertainty". If you are facing illness of any kind or difficulties, whether it be physical or struggles of the heart, what she has to share will make a big difference in your life. Rhonda is an inspiration!

JEFF CAVINS FOUNDER, *The Great Adventure!*

With heartfelt openness, Rhonda shines a light on carrying her cross that casts an encouraging and healing shadow on those who find themselves struggling under the weight of their own crosses. Rhonda's journey through the valleys and peaks that accompany a cancer diagnosis is not the path she planned, yet she finds that God has equipped her for anything she encounters. In sharing her story, Rhonda helps us better live our story, teaching us that when each step is taken in faith and each moment is trusted to the Lord, then every day is an opportunity to walk in joy. This book is a blessing—no matter where you are on your own journey.

KELLY WAHLQUIST *Founder of*
WINE: Women In the New Evangelization
Author, Created to Relate: God's Design for Peace and Joy

With deep faith, sincerity, and humor, Rhonda Zweber offers a personal glimpse of facing and fighting cancer. Accepting this cross has molded her into more than a survivor; she is a cancer thriver. Open the pages of this book, a gift, grace, and blessing, to pray with her and to be inspired to take up your cross, whatever it may be.

URSULINE SISTER BRIDGET HAASE *Missionary, Author,*
Sister Storyteller. (www.wisdomwonder.com)

DEDICATION

To my heavenly Father who placed upon my heart to write this book and who walked with me every step of the way.

To my husband Val; our daughters Ashley, Hailey and Sally; our sons-in-law Danny and Alex, who have made our family life extraordinary and ordinary at the same time and who have loved me through the difficult times and the everyday moments.

Contents

Introduction

"A sower went out to sow his seed; and as he sowed, some fell on the path and was trampled on, and the birds of the air ate it up. Some fell on the rock; and as it grew up, it withered for lack of moisture. Some fell among thorns, and the thorns grew with it and choked it. Some fell into good soil, and when it grew, it produced a hundredfold." As he said this, he called out, "Let anyone with ears to hear listen!"

Then his disciples asked him what this parable meant. He said, "To you it has been given to know the secrets of the kingdom of God; but to others I speak in parables, so that

'looking they may not perceive, and listening they may not understand.'

"Now the parable is this: The seed is the word of God. The ones on the path are those who have heard; then the devil comes and takes away the word from their hearts, so that they may not believe and be saved. The ones on the rock are those who, when they hear the word, receive it with joy. But these have no root; they believe only for a while and in a time of testing fall away. As for what fell among the thorns, these are the ones who hear; but as they go on their way, they are choked by the cares and riches and pleasures of life, and their fruit does not mature. But as for that in the good soil, these are the ones who, when they hear the word, hold it fast in an honest and good heart, and bear fruit with patient endurance." (Luke 8:5-15)

I EXPERIENCED LIVING ON ROCKY GROUND after I graduated from college and was living in Florida. I hadn't attended Mass regularly throughout my college years but finally felt moved by the Holy Spirit to do so. I found a Catholic church and began going to Sunday Mass pretty consistently. I was

1

listening to the Gospel and felt good when I left Mass, but as the week wore on what I had heard on Sunday went right out the window with the warm Florida breeze.

My "thorny" stage was when my husband, Val, and I had gotten married and our family began to grow. Along with the birth of three daughters, I thought the "good life" was having a big house, a new car, vacations, and many more of the material pleasures of our culture. What came with that life was the racing around, driving the girls to their activities. There were days that would pass by and I couldn't remember what I accomplished. We were attending Mass each Sunday and yet I was still not getting much out of it because I didn't know what I was searching for.

I now realize that I was missing a personal relationship with my heavenly Father. I had absolutely no doubt that He existed but I barely even knew Him. I prayed very little unless it was during Mass or before meals. I would thank Him every now and then, but I didn't understand the magnitude of His generosity in order to give Him the Glory in which He deserves.

My cancer diagnosis changed that.

Out of nowhere, while waiting for test results, God placed a simple prayer on my heart. "Thy will be done, just give me the strength to get through it." Those words surprised me with an inner peace I could not have imagined feeling with such life changing news. This peace has helped navigate me through life ever since.

After my diagnosis, I felt that God wanted me to share my journey as I carried my cross of cancer, to encourage others as they carried their own cross; whether it was an illness, the death of a loved one, or the loss of a job. Everyone has some kind of cross that they must carry. For many years now, I feel I have done just that. But, it wasn't until I met with my spiritual director, that I realized more than anything, that God wanted me to share the joy I have found in developing my beautiful relationship with Him. Cancer was the vehicle—clunker that it is—that drove me to truly know Him.

I find joy in each and every day, even though it may be difficult on some days. I feel peace as I continue to live with stage 4 metastatic breast cancer that has moved throughout my bones and digestive system. I have faith that God will lead me home when my work here is done. And, I know that my soil is becoming richer each day that I include God in it. My hope is that you can find joy, peace and faith throughout your life's journey, too. My hope is that your soil is rich and fertile or will begin to become rich and fertile after reading this book, so that you can produce a great abundance of fruit.

Reading Between the Signs was written for anyone who has a cross to carry and is searching for someone or something to help them get through it. That someone is Jesus and that something is His loving Presence. I hope that as you read the stories, you can place yourself in the story and see how walking with Jesus can help you on your journey.

Although, being diagnosed with cancer unlocked my heart to pursue a relationship with Jesus, it is not what this book is about. Throughout my treatment plan, Jesus provided the road-map for me to walk with Him. I came to trust Him completely. This book is about how my faith has grown throughout all of the trials and tribulations that God has strategically placed in my life to bring me closer to Him. It will explain how I began to understand that by keeping God close during the good times, I could trust in Him during the difficult times, allowing me to relax in His love at all times.

Along with the trust I have in Him, God has encouraged me to accept whatever plan He has for me. He put those words on my heart from the very beginning of my cancer journey and I pray that I can recognize what He wants me to do for HIM. He places many opportunities in our lives for us to serve Him. We just need to learn to recognize the signs He places before us in our daily life and fulfill His will for us.

I hope that the scripture readings that you have heard over the years come to life, your life, as I relate them to the experiences I have had as I continue to carry my cross. My reflections come from reading scripture, inspirational books, and daily devotionals; listening to holy men and women talk about our Catholic faith, and many Holy Spirit moments that I have been blessed with.

So, come along with me on my journey—one that includes miracle mountain top experiences, lonely and sad walks through the desert (or wilderness?), and many peaceful rest stops along the way.

> *Happy moments, praise God. Difficult moments, seek God. Quiet moments, worship God. Painful moments, trust God. Every moment, thank God.*

Acknowledgments

W E ARE ALL ON DIFFERENT PATHS IN LIFE. Some are traveling toward Jesus and some are traveling away from Jesus. Some may even be stuck, not knowing which way to walk. God loves every one of us, right where we are but His desire is for each of us to be moving closer to Him.

We have a choice to make. Do we want to receive the graces and blessings that God is offering us? Do we want peace and joy in our lives? Do we want to know the fullness of God's love and the truth in His words? My answer to all of these questions is a great big Mary 'YES'!

When I said yes to God's call for me to write this book, I put everything into His hands. I didn't know how it would all play out but trusted that He would provide me with whatever I needed to accomplish His will for me. I began writing and took every sign from God that I thought was guiding me in the right direction. I counted on our Blessed Mother to also guide me in my words and actions.

I want to take this opportunity to thank those who have helped this book come to fruition.

To my family, friends and the many, many prayer warriors who have sustained me from the very beginning of my journey and for those who have joined me along the way. I believe your prayers are a big reason why I'm still here today! Thank you!

To my dear friends, DeAnne Shea and Maggie Stack, who helped me get the words from my heart to my head and to the paper. Thank you for allowing me to pour out my deepest thoughts all over you.

To my doctors and nurses in the Cancer Center at St. Francis Hospital who have cared for me over the years. Your kindness and compassion and patience have been remarkable even when I try to evangelize while you are trying to treat me!

For those who are suffering and for those who have gone on to eternal rest. Thank you for showing me God's mercy and grace and for the privilege to pray for you. May your reward in Heaven be great.

To my brother in law, Bob Beck, whose artistic talent I wanted to share with others through illustrations of the each chapter. They are amazing!

To my friend, Alyssa Bormes who suggested I contact Dale Ahlquist to see if he would be interested in publishing the book. Thank you, Alyssa, for being the voice of Christ, and leading me to Dale.

Finally, to Dale Ahlquist. I've gotten to know Dale, first as the co-founder of Chesterton Academy, since my daughter Sally is a student there and now, as my publisher. When I sent Dale my transcript, I had no idea how much he knew about my journey. I think I surprised him. He told me during our first conversation after reading it that my story wasn't finished yet and to keep on writing. Dale, your words of encouragement has affirmed my mission for God. I know He is pleased with your role in His plan for me. Thank you for taking a chance on me, especially since my story isn't quite like G.K. Chesterton's.

Foreword

BY DALE AHLQUIST

THE ROAD THROUGH LIFE IS NEVER PREDICTABLE. The only thing we can expect is the unexpected. That is not only what this story is about; it is the story of how the story came about.

When Rhonda Zweber walked into my office and said she was writing a book—and when she told me what it was about—I was a little doubtful. No, that's not true. I was completely doubtful. I was doubtful that the story would be any good, and I was doubtful that I would be the one to publish it. I publish only three or four titles a year and they usually have something to do with G.K. Chesterton. Surprisingly, that is actually a broad category, but I knew that Rhonda's book was not going to fall within it. I was sympathetic, and for all the right reasons, but I was doubtful.

Then I read it.

Not only was I drawn in immediately, I was transfixed. Not only did she take me with her on her journey, she touched my soul. I was moved. I was edified. I was in awe. This is an amazing, incredible story. And how, I asked myself, could this woman go through all these things and be so joyful? This is a first hand account of grace. As I read it, I was thinking to myself, "Somebody should publish this!" Then I remembered that I was a publisher, and that was, in fact, why I was reading it. That's how lost in it I was.

G.K. Chesterton—whom this book is not about—referred to one book of the Bible more than all the others: the Book of

Job, the ancient poem about the riddle of suffering. "Why?" we ask. "Why, why, why? Why do these things happen?" Job asked the question. We all ask the question. And Chesterton reflects: "The refusal of God to explain His design is itself a burning hint of His design." The road of faith is the greatest adventure. We don't know what waits around the corner.

Most people think they've read the Book of Job, but they haven't. They think they know the story, but they don't. They avoid reading it the same way they avoid suffering. That's understandable. But they rob themselves of the lesson they need to know when the time comes.

This is another book that people might be tempted to avoid. I remember trying to avoid it myself. But someday they will need it, or someone they love will need it, or someone they don't even know will need it. They will need this book. They will be helped by it, inspired by it, blessed by it. If their body does not experience healing, their soul will.

One of the most surprising lessons—one that Rhonda explains better than I will here—is that life doesn't stop even when life seems to be stopping. Even when everything is completely collapsing, there are details to attend to. It is one of the many things that doesn't seem fair. And yet, our duties serve the salubrious purpose of helping us take our eyes off ourselves and keeping them on the road ahead.

When Rhonda walked in and said she was writing a book, she also said she hadn't finished it. Another reason for me to be doubtful. When I told her I was going to publish it, she got back to work writing it, and the story of her journey just kept getting more fascinating. But as you will see, she still hasn't finished writing it. Nobody gets to write the last chapter of their own story.

Two Roads Diverged

WHILE WAITING FOR RESULTS of an ultrasound on my breast, I was lying on the exam table and words from a familiar prayer came to my mind, "*Thy will be done*." Then, I asked for the strength to get through whatever "Thy will" was. Within just seconds, the radiologist walked into the room and gently told me that she didn't like what she saw on the ultrasound and wanted to perform a needle biopsy of my breast.

The biopsy results took a couple of days. The waiting was terrible to endure, but that was just the beginning of the realization that I was not in control. I kept busy during those days and finally, when I couldn't wait any longer for the phone call from my family doctor, I called his office and was told that my message would get to him as soon as possible. At 11:59 am, Friday, May 18, 2007, the phone rang and changed my life.

There were tears, of course. I heard my doctor's words confirming that I had breast cancer, yet I was not panicked in any way, I was actually calm. I had a couple of days to prepare myself for the possibility of the diagnosis. My husband, Val, walked into the room. I gave him the "thumbs down" sign. After listening to the plan that my doctor was telling me, I hung up the phone and went straight into Val's arms and he held me close and we both cried. I remember our youngest daughter, Sally, then only four years old, wanting to get in on the hug, not having any idea what had just happened. All three of us held each other for a few minutes, in silence. Sally's presence was a grace given to us so our focus would be taken off of the devastating news we had just received and focus on the gift of our family.

Another grace we were blessed with was the few hours we had that allowed us to process and accept what the doctor told us before our older daughters, Ashley, age 12 and Hailey, age 10, came home from school. They knew we would have the results by then and they had convinced themselves that I did not have cancer. What a great assurance that they thought about a positive outcome, rather than a negative one. As the girls walked into the house, Hailey cut to the chase and asked, "So, do you have cancer?" I'm sure she was certain that she already knew the answer. We told the girls it wasn't the news we had hoped for but we believed that everything would be ok. And it *was* ok. I needed to be the same mom that I was before that phone call. Just like any other school day, I asked the girls if they had homework to do; I fixed dinner for the family; and we all went to watch Hailey play her soccer game. One more grace on that day was the ability to set aside the unsettling news and continue on with life as usual. If we weren't given this grace, I believe we would have sat at home and felt sorry for ourselves and been overwhelmed with the possibilities that lie ahead of us.

But immediately Jesus spoke to them and said, "Take heart, it is I; do not be afraid."

Peter answered him, "Lord, if it is you, command me to come to you on the water." He said, "Come." So Peter got out of the boat, started walking on the water, and came toward Jesus. But when he noticed the strong wind, he became frightened, and beginning to sink, he cried out, "Lord, save me!" Jesus immediately reached out his hand and caught him, saying to him, "You of little faith, why did you doubt?" (Matthew 14:27-31)

I was Peter, sitting in the boat that was being tossed around with the news of my diagnosis. Like Peter, I was being asked to take a leap of faith and step out of my comfortable life; the big house, Sunday Mass, good Catholic family; and trust Jesus, by walking towards Him on a sea of uncertainty and during this very scary and unsettling time of my life. Of course, I didn't know that then because I didn't know Jesus very well, then. Yet, the calm I felt surprised me. I never cried out, "Lord, save me," like Peter did. I never even asked Him, "Why me?"

I believe that God was preparing me for my journey without me paying any attention. He was working on my heart, filling it with trust and faith, waiting for me to accept His will for me. To this day, I am still amazed at how easily I accepted my cross. Yes, I had days when my feet would get wet from sinking ever so slightly, doubting God's Presence. But, then I grabbed His hand and knew His love would sustain me.

The first days after hearing devastating news can be very confusing, scary, frustrating and many more emotions that are all natural to feel. Sometimes, all it takes to get through those days is to take one step at a time, do what needs to be done and just breathe. You may just be surprised at how you are able to handle the news. You may not have realized it, but Jesus was right beside you!

Walk by Faith and not by Sight

2 CORINTHIANS 5:7

Angels Light the Way

Meanwhile Saul, still breathing threats and murder against the disciples of the Lord, went to the high priest and asked him for letters to the synagogues at Damascus, so that if he found any who belonged to the Way, men or women, he might bring them bound to Jerusalem. Now as he was going along and approaching Damascus, suddenly a light from heaven flashed around him. He fell to the ground and heard a voice saying to him, "Saul, Saul, why do you persecute me?" He asked, "Who are you, Lord?" The reply came, "I am Jesus, whom you are persecuting. But get up and enter the city, and you will be told what you are to do." The men who were traveling with him stood speechless because they heard the voice but saw no one. Saul got up from the ground, and though his eyes were open, he could see nothing; so they led him by the hand and brought him into Damascus. For three days he was without sight, and neither ate nor drank.

Now there was a disciple in Damascus named Ananias. The Lord said to him in a vision, "Ananias." He answered, "Here I am, Lord." The Lord said to him, "Get up and go to the street called Straight, and at the house of Judas look for a man of Tarsus named Saul. At this moment he is praying, and he has seen in a vision a man named Ananias come in and lay his hands on him so that he might regain his sight." But Ananias answered, "Lord, I have heard from many about this man, how much evil he has done to your saints in Jerusalem; and here he has authority from the chief priests to bind all who invoke your name." But the Lord said to him, "Go, for he is an instrument whom I have chosen to bring my name before Gentiles and kings and before the people of Israel; I myself will show him how much he must suffer for the sake of my name." So Ananias went and entered the house. He laid his hands on Saul and said, "Brother Saul, the Lord Jesus, who appeared to you on your way here, has sent me so that you may regain your sight and be filled with the Holy Spirit." And immediately something like scales fell from his eyes, and his sight was restored. Then he got up and was baptized, and after taking some food, he regained his strength. (Acts 9:1-19)

How many times have you seen something over and over again, and then one day, the "scales fall from your eyes" and you see the situation in a totally different light? Jesus is the one who "opened" my eyes at Sunday Mass, just two days after being diagnosed with breast cancer. As I looked around the church, something absolutely amazing happened. As you can imagine, I was still processing the news of my diagnosis and I had many thoughts going through my mind, but then, there was a peace that came over me. There were light beams shining down on the women in our faith community that had gone through breast cancer before me. Literally, light shining on them! And they weren't sitting by each other, they were scattered around the sanctuary. I looked to see where the sun was located at that time of the morning and it was shining outside but this source of the light was not coming from that sun. I believe that God sent His angels to point out to me, those women who would be there for me, as I began my journey. The light was like the flash of light that caused Saul to fall. The scales on my eyes did not allow me to see these women before that moment as breast cancer survivors, and certainly had no understanding of what they had gone through. I've seen these women, Sunday after Sunday, and some I saw more often, but until I was diagnosed, I had not given them much thought or concern. I felt and still feel a little ashamed about that, but it has given me a new appreciation of supporting others on their journey through difficult times.

When the Holy Spirit filled Saul, he began to turn his life around and, as we know, he became one of the greatest Apostles. Without realizing it at that time, The Holy Spirit opened my eyes and my heart (remember when I was lying on the table after my ultrasound?) and I began to see life differently. And, like Saul, I continue to share my commitment to Jesus.

Those first days after receiving the news of a new cross to carry, we are still sorting out what has just happened. For some, Jesus and His mercy isn't the first thing that comes to our minds; it may take a while before our eyes are open to seeing the blessings of our cross.

Your word is a lamp to my feet
and a light to my path.

Psalm 119:105

Start Your Engines!

W ITH MY PORT PLACED just the day before, the incision was still fresh and I thought it would hurt when the IV was put in for my first chemo treatment. I was pleasantly surprised that it didn't hurt any more than if a regular IV was put in, actually it was better than a regular IV. Administering the chemo would take a couple of hours and I knew that, so I brought things to do, including my Journal and a book to read. Of course, Val was there right by my side to chat with me yet we did nothing but hang out and watch the personal TV next to my comfy chair on the first day. Because the meds made me feel relaxed, almost sleepy, I had my eyes closed a lot of the time.

On the 10 minute drive home from the hospital, I mentioned to Val, that I felt like I had two margaritas (my limit), and had a little buzz, if you will. We chuckled. Within minutes,

I added that I felt that I just had another margarita (over my limit!)! It wasn't and icky feeling, just a bit loopy! When we got home, I had a little lunch and went up to my bedroom where I spent most of the rest of the day, sleeping.

So, the first day of chemo turned out to be pretty good. It was nothing like I thought it would be. I thought that as soon as I received the toxic drugs I would be miserable and be vomiting until I finished with the months of treatments. I was so wrong! I had no nausea, a little discomfort from my port placement, a little headache, and a little buzz. Again, everybody reacts differently to chemotherapy and I was blessed to feel as well as I did.

> *Therefore I tell you, do not worry about your life, what you will eat or what you will drink, or about your body, what you will wear. Is not life more than food, and the body more than clothing? Look at the birds of the air; they neither sow nor reap nor gather into barns, and yet your heavenly Father feeds them. Are you not of more value than they? And can any of you by worrying add a single hour to your span of life? And why do you worry about clothing? Consider the lilies of the field, how they grow; they neither toil nor spin, yet I tell you, even Solomon in all his glory was not clothed like one of these. But if God so clothes the grass of the field, which is alive today and tomorrow is thrown into the oven, will he not much more clothe you—you of little faith? Therefore do not worry, saying, 'What will we eat?' or 'What will we drink?' or 'What will we wear?' For it is the Gentiles who strive for all these things; and indeed your heavenly Father knows that you need all these things. But strive first for the kingdom of God and his righteousness, and all these things will be given to you as well.*
>
> *So do not worry about tomorrow, for tomorrow will bring worries of its own. Today's trouble is enough for today. (Matthew 6:25-34)*

The next day was another story. I woke up early feeling sick to my stomach and thought, "here we go." I took one of the

Winding Road Ahead

Like a shepherd He feeds his flock and gathers the lambs in His arms, holding them carefully close to His heart, leading them home.

I myself will shepherd them, for others have led them astray. The lost I will rescue and heal their wounds and pasture them, giving them rest. Come unto me if you are heavily burdened, and take my yoke upon your shoulders. I will give you rest. (Song written by Bob Dufford, inspired by Isaiah 40:11)

THE IMAGE OF JESUS with the small lamb lying across his shoulders is what I envision when I sing this Psalm. His tender and loving care for me gives me such peace. There are times in our lives that we may feel like a lost sheep, wandering in no particular direction. At those times, we can call out to our Shepherd and ask for Him to lead us back to His arms. Jesus, as the Good Shepherd, also assures me that He is always with me, guarding me from danger.

I love to go to the thrift stores and walk up and down the isles, searching for the perfect find. One day I found a figurine of Jesus sitting on a rock with a lamb on His lap. I picked it up and smiled as I imagined being that tiny sheep being held gently in His arms. I stood there for several minutes deciding if I should buy the figurine. We had just moved into our townhome and had gotten rid of many things. I was really trying not to add to what we had, but I really wanted Jesus.

I struggled with myself for a few more minutes and decided to put the figurine back on the shelf for someone else to enjoy. I regretted that decision as soon as I got home and read the readings for the day. It was one of the many that speaks of Jesus being the Good Shepherd! I went so far as to go back to the thrift store and try to find it. It had been a few days before I was able to get there and I couldn't find it. I even asked the owner, if she remembered selling it. I was so disappointed. That figurine was the perfect depiction of what I imagine Jesus is as our Shepherd—tender and loving. I hope I find another figurine like that someday.

I was scheduled to meet with my oncologist on the same day of Ashley's 13th birthday. If I had a choice, I would not have chosen my appointment to be on that day. Turning 13 is a big deal, especially for girls and especially for my girl. I thought Ashley was handling the change in our lives pretty well, but I soon realized that she was doing her best to keep a smile on her face whenever she was with me, so that I wouldn't worry about her.

I had planned a surprise party for her with a few friends, but I was a little concerned about how the day would play out. Her surprise party had been planned long before I learned what kind of surprise party God had planned for me.

As it was, my appointment with my oncologist was very lengthy and Val and I received a lot of information about what our lives were going to be like, and honestly, we felt quite overwhelmed. Even though God knew exactly what my journey looked like, I had no idea what I would encounter on the winding road ahead of me. But I knew that I had to listen and accept what we were being told and accept God's plan for me. It was amazing how much there was to know about the cross that I was about to carry and how long I would have to carry it! I brought a journal to document my journey and handed it right over to Val to take notes. I wanted to focus on just listening to what the doctor said while Val took notes. Bringing a notebook of some kind to doctor's appointments is something I always suggest people to do. It's also very useful to jot down questions you may want to ask the doctor at your next visit. The doctor explained the details of treatment for the next six years! The plan was laid out for us, with chemotherapy starting within just days, but not before several more appointments that needed to be taken care of. I had an ultrasound of my heart because the chemotherapy drugs would be very powerful and could possibly damage my heart, so the ultrasound would document the baseline for my heart. I also needed a bone scan, CT scan of my abdomen and upper body, and a CT scan of my head. The following day was the day I dreaded the most up until that point. It was the day that I needed to have my port placed to be used to administer my chemo without destroying my veins. Without skipping a beat, I would begin my chemo the very next day, and I would have chemo every other week for the next eight weeks. The type of chemo I would have, very likely, would cause my hair to fall out. We were told that I needed to have genetic testing done at some time in the future in order to know if there is a higher risk of getting cancer for our daughters and my siblings. Talk about a crazy roadmap! Just writing every-thing that happened in those first few days makes my head spin! Suddenly, our world was moving at high speed and I needed to get control of my racing thoughts before I crashed, even before I began this race for my life.

It was the first time I actually felt sad. I began to cry on the way home from my appointment, but then I realized that I didn't have to do anything but enjoy Ashley's party that day. I didn't need to make any important decisions regarding my health. All I needed to do was to be the mother sheep that my family needed me to be.

And Ashley's surprise party? It was wonderful and I even surprised myself by being able to pull it off!

I will not leave you or forsake you.

JOSHUA 1:5

Pack Your Bags

THERE I WAS, ABOUT TO EMBARK on a path that I never thought I would travel. I didn't doubt for a moment that I would survive what was ahead of me, but I was trying to imagine what I needed for my trip. If I were planning a vacation to Florida, I would easily be able to make a checklist of what to bring: shorts, t-shirts, sunscreen, and flip flops. But, how could I prepare for this?

Then Jesus called the twelve together and gave them power and authority over all demons and to cure diseases, and he sent them out to proclaim the kingdom of God and to heal. He said to them, "Take nothing for your journey, no staff, nor bag, nor bread, nor money—not even an extra tunic. Whatever house you enter, stay there, and leave from there. Wherever they do not welcome you, as you are leaving that town shake the dust off your feet as a testimony against them." They departed and went through the villages, bringing the good news and curing diseases everywhere. (Luke 9:1-6)

Jesus told his apostles to take nothing for their journey. No food, money, or even a clean set of clothes. Why did He do this? He wanted the apostles to know that all they needed was God. God would give them whatever they needed, wherever they went. Always. If they could put their total trust in God, that would be enough, and it was enough. They proved that by following God's lead and responding by being faithful to Him, He provided whatever they were lacking, whether is was nourishment or encouragement.

God can help us believe that we can do anything, too, as long as we have faith and trust in Him like the apostles did. Before I was diagnosed, I would see someone going through cancer and think to myself that there was no way *I* could ever fight cancer. I am very thankful that God never thought that of me. His love led me to believe that I *could* fight cancer, AND I AM STILL FIGHTING!

God has created us for His purpose, and we need to be able to see that in ourselves. We need to believe that the gifts we have been given are to be put to good use and not just stored away in our hearts. God will develop those gifts and talents and if we ask, He will show us how to use them for His Glory. Jesus prepares us for each day, knowing exactly what will happen but we only wish we knew exactly what each day has in store for us. So, in my spiritual suitcase, I packed determination to get through whatever I needed to because I was a wife, mother, daughter, sister, and a friend, and I didn't plan on going any-where anytime soon, I wanted to add grandmother to these titles, too. I packed the trust that surprised me on the exam table that God would take care of me, even though I wasn't quite sure what that really meant at that time. I packed hope that my treatment plan would kill the cancer in my body and that I would be able to handle the side effects. And I packed a lot of prayers from my family and friends. Wow! The amount of prayers that I received could have filled several suitcases! Prayers for me and my family have been so powerful. From the very beginning, I received prayers from our community and some from people I had never met. That was an amazing feeling, knowing that I was 'covered' in the prayer department. But, as amazing at it was, it didn't make me want to pray anymore than I did before my diagnosis. Although, my heart and my eyes had been opened, it would still take some time for me to understand how important it was for me to include prayer into my daily routine.

I wasn't sure if I had packed enough of anything, but it was enough to get me moving forward. Along the way, I picked up a few priceless souvenirs: joy, peace, and many blessings and tucked them into the side pockets of my spiritual suitcase. I also gained a Traveling Companion who took over the driver's seat, which meant that I could sit shotgun, spend a lot of time with Him and, amazingly, enjoy the ride!

Cast all your worries upon Him.

1 PETER 5:7

Billboard Signs

ONE OF THE TOUGHEST DAYS I think Hailey experienced, was the day I decided to shave my head before all of my hair fell out. We went as a family to see my hairstylist, because I wanted them to be part of that life-changing event.

With Val and our three girls surrounding me, I sat in the chair and my stylist started out by giving me a Mohawk! We all laughed. As each swipe of the electric razor took off a row of my hair, I was seeing in the mirror before me a change in my looks and with it, a change in my expression. It didn't take long before my head was completely shaved. I looked at all of my hair on the floor and looked back into the mirror of the image that the world would now see, like a giant billboard sign, and

I wasn't laughing anymore. Neither was Hailey. She had been standing nearby, very quiet and just taking it all in. It was the first outward sign that something had changed in our lives. In fact, that is one of the things I learned quickly; cancer is a family disease. Like many of the crosses we carry, everyone is affected.

My focus turned toward Hailey and what she may have been thinking. Was she going to be bothered by my looks or by the looks that I would get, now that I, quite noticeably, looked different? Being just ten years old, I imagined the reaction of others could be difficult for her to understand.

When we got home, Hailey went right up to her bedroom. I wanted to let her know it was ok to feel mad or sad or however she felt. I went up and asked if I could come in and talk. We had a good conversation and she and I cried for a little bit as she shared her fears of the unknown territory we entered. I'm glad Hailey was able to share her feelings with me and this was the first of many close moments we would have together.

The hair loss wasn't really an issue for me and it really wasn't even an issue for our family but I know that isn't the case for everyone and I know that I need to be sensitive about that. The girls were even involved in taking turns at shaving my head, just days after the buzz cut that I got from my stylist. Hailey had fun drawing hearts and smiley faces through the shaving cream on my head before she shaved away the last of my hair. With the exception of wanting to know when to expect my hair to fall out, I really didn't mind being bald. There were actually many times when I was thrilled that I didn't have to 'do my hair.' I always liked a low maintenance hairstyle, and being bald was maintenance free! I was given many adorable caps and hats and scarves by friends and I enjoyed having so many to choose from when I left the house. Most of the time at home, I didn't wear anything. In the very beginning, I would walk past a mirror and catch my reflection and be surprised that I had forgotten that I had no hair!

As my hair began to grow back after all of my chemotherapy treatments were done, I remember the morning that I woke up with bed head. You know, when your hair is so messed up that you definitely have to do something with it before leaving the house? Well, my bed head wasn't THAT noticeable, but there were a few tiny little hairs that were bent and leaning in a different direction of the other tiny hairs! I was so excited!

Throughout the Bible, lepers were considered unclean, both physically and spiritually. They were sent to live alone in secluded areas. People thought that leprosy fell upon anyone who had sinned against God. We know that isn't true. Our God is not like that. (I think it is spread by a bacteria, which could be as a result of unsanitary conditions, but also via human contact.)

Lepers were looked upon with such disgust due to the disfigurement the diseased caused, and were not allowed to come within six feet of others, including their families. Can you imagine how those children of God felt as they were shunned from their own family? The looks they got from others, not understanding what they did to deserve this?

He left that place and came to his hometown, and his disciples followed him. On the sabbath he began to teach in the synagogue, and many who heard him were astounded. They said, "Where did this man get all this? What is this wisdom that has been given to him? What deeds of power are being done by his hands! Is not this the carpenter, the son of Mary and brother of James and Joses and Judas and Simon, and are not his sisters here with us?" And they took offense at him. Then Jesus said to them, "Prophets are not without honor, except in their hometown, and among their own kin, and in their own house." And he could do no deed of power there, except that he laid his hands on a few sick people and cured them. And he was amazed at their unbelief. (Mark 6:1-6)

Jesus must have felt like a leper when he returned to his hometown of Nazareth to teach in the synagogue. Even though the people of Nazareth were astounded at what Jesus said, they soon began to question the words that Jesus spoke since he was known as a simple carpenter and the son of Mary. Then Jesus said to them, "Prophets are not without honor, except in their hometown, and among their own kin, and in their own house." Since Jesus was not accepted among the people who he grew up with, it was very difficult but He still healed sick people and was "amazed at their unbelief".

This is a dramatic comparison to what Hailey may have felt, but it does represent the feeling of me standing out among our community, with a bald head and wondering what others would think. I didn't look like that because I had sinned (although, I am a sinner) but I did get looks of great pity at the sight of my obvious change in appearance. I experienced, from those who felt sorry for me, avoidance of eye contact and conversation. I was that way before cancer and I understand the feeling of not knowing what to say, but after experiencing being "shunned", I don't avoid those who are noticeably going through some type of suffering anymore. In fact, I ask the Holy Spirit to give me opportunities to reach out to those people in order for them NOT to feel like a leper.

Let the Spirit change your way of thinking.

EPHESIANS 4:23

Start Your Engines!

WITH MY PORT PLACED just the day before, the incision was still fresh and I thought it would hurt when the IV was put in for my first chemo treatment. I was pleasantly surprised that it didn't hurt any more than if a regular IV was put in, actually it was better than a regular IV. Administering the chemo would take a couple of hours and I knew that, so I brought things to do, including my Journal and a book to read. Of course, Val was there right by my side to chat with me yet we did nothing but hang out and watch the personal TV next to my comfy chair on the first day. Because the meds made me feel relaxed, almost sleepy, I had my eyes closed a lot of the time.

On the 10 minute drive home from the hospital, I mentioned to Val, that I felt like I had two margaritas (my limit), and had a little buzz, if you will. We chuckled. Within minutes,

I added that I felt that I just had another margarita (over my limit!)! It wasn't and icky feeling, just a bit loopy! When we got home, I had a little lunch and went up to my bedroom where I spent most of the rest of the day, sleeping.

So, the first day of chemo turned out to be pretty good. It was nothing like I thought it would be. I thought that as soon as I received the toxic drugs I would be miserable and be vomiting until I finished with the months of treatments. I was so wrong! I had no nausea, a little discomfort from my port placement, a little headache, and a little buzz. Again, everybody reacts differently to chemotherapy and I was blessed to feel as well as I did.

Therefore I tell you, do not worry about your life, what you will eat or what you will drink, or about your body, what you will wear. Is not life more than food, and the body more than clothing? Look at the birds of the air; they neither sow nor reap nor gather into barns, and yet your heavenly Father feeds them. Are you not of more value than they? And can any of you by worrying add a single hour to your span of life? And why do you worry about clothing? Consider the lilies of the field, how they grow; they neither toil nor spin, yet I tell you, even Solomon in all his glory was not clothed like one of these. But if God so clothes the grass of the field, which is alive today and tomorrow is thrown into the oven, will he not much more clothe you—you of little faith? Therefore do not worry, saying, 'What will we eat?' or 'What will we drink?' or 'What will we wear?' For it is the Gentiles who strive for all these things; and indeed your heavenly Father knows that you need all these things. But strive first for the kingdom of God and his righteousness, and all these things will be given to you as well.

So do not worry about tomorrow, for tomorrow will bring worries of its own. Today's trouble is enough for today. (Matthew 6:25-34)

The next day was another story. I woke up early feeling sick to my stomach and thought, "here we go." I took one of the prescribed anti-nausea pills and fell back asleep. I felt yucky pretty much all day but it never was too bad. I still didn't want to do much but lie in bed and sleep all day. I took each day as it came. There were days when I did very little and there were days when I felt really good. I was very blessed to have had only had a handful of icky days throughout my journey with chemotherapy. I knew what my job was and it was to receive my chemo, "do the work" and let Jesus do the rest. I was beginning to see what this Bible passage meant. Live today and don't worry about tomorrow. How many times have we heard that phrase? I was starting to live it.

Be strong and courageous, and do the work.

1 Chronicles 28:20

Extended Road Trip

AFTER MY FOUR ROUNDS of chemotherapy, I was scheduled for a lumpectomy, surgery to remove the tumor from my breast. I had been posting updates on my CaringBridge site and after my surgery, Val posted this for me:

Hello all,

This is Val writing for my beautiful wife. Her surgery went well and as planned. The doctor performed a lumpectomy and also took out three lymph nodes. (I had to ask Rhonda how to spell those fancy words). What that means is they removed the tumor, a whopper, according to the doctor, and some other important string things that she wanted to get further tested. We will find out by Friday on the results and keep you updated.

What I (Val) have learned living with a loved one who has cancer: 1) It's scary, especially in the beginning. 2) My three *daughters are great help and support to Rhonda. 3) I take good health for granted. 4) Cancer patients can get mad at their family and vice versa, although the make up time is quicker. 5) Rhonda is a huge inspiration to me and many others. And finally, I am amazed by the love and support that we continuously receive from our family, friends and community. Thank you for checking this site, your prayers, meals, driving our kids and keeping them overnight, cards, emails and phone calls. We are truly blessed!*

When my Cancer Care Coordinator called me the day after my lumpectomy, I thought it was so nice of her to check in to see how I was feeling. She asked how I was doing but that wasn't the only reason for the phone call. She told me that the results of the surgery weren't as good as my surgeon had hoped they would be. The surgeon actually took 10 lymph nodes out and nine of them tested positive for cancer, but that wasn't all. The tumor was removed but the margins were not clear. Those were the stringy things that Val mentioned in his post. That meant that they did not get all of the cancer cells during surgery, so my surgeon strongly encouraged me to have my entire breast removed.

I was completely numb.

Even though we were given all of the possibilities of what might be found once the doctor had opened me up, I still remained positive that all would be fine with just a lumpectomy. This news actually hit me harder than the original phone call telling me about my diagnosis. Thankfully, Val was home and got on the other phone to listen because my mind was completely blank and I wasn't able to hear anything. My little "bump in the road" of life changed in that moment. My road trip just got extended.

Again, Val said everything would be okay. I just needed to trust him which I did. Trust was something that came automatically with my diagnosis, somehow God had given me the grace to trust Him. No matter what happened if I believed that God loved me so much and if I let myself be filled with His love and there would be no room for fear, I knew I would be okay and the prayers and love that I received from my family and friends, which really made a difference in my attitude, would sustain me as I ventured into unknown territory once again.

When Jesus was in the Garden of Gethsemane, he pleaded, "Father, if you are willing, take this cup from me; yet not my will, but yours be done." When we are faced with fear, do we cry out to God? Can we accept God's will for us, even if it means to carry the heavy burden of the cross? Jesus wants us to cry out to Him, ask Him for whatever we need to get through tough times. By doing this, our relationship with Him will deepen and we will be open to receive peace and acceptance. Then, there will less room in our heart for fear.

Say to those whose hearts are frightened: be strong fear not!

Isaiah 35:4

Walking Through the Desert

INSTEAD OF HAVING ONE BREAST REMOVED, I chose to have both removed and that surgery was scheduled a couple of weeks after my lumpectomy. Our family had planned a vacation and we wanted to be able to enjoy it before my surgery, which we greatly did.

After my double mastectomy, Val posted again on my CaringBridge site:

Hello Everyone,
This is Val with the update. I just got back with the girls from visiting Rhonda. The surgery went well. It took just under two hours. Rhonda felt a bit queasy soon after she woke up. She is doing fine now, very tired, so we did not stay long. She will spend the night in the hospital tonight and come home sometime on Thursday.

I'm sure Rhonda will let you know her feelings tomorrow on how she initially feels with the change. We did not really talk about it too much since she wasn't totally 100%. I know she will probably be a little sad, I know I am right now. The continued support certainly helps all of us.

Thank you for keeping us in your prayers, Val

Waking up after my double mastectomy surgery was a lot different than any other surgery I've had. Val's post was a little understated; I felt awful. I was nauseous and my head wasn't clear from the anesthesia when I saw the girls. Val had gone home to get them so they could see me and they were with me for less than 10 minutes because I felt so sick. I managed to give them a smile to make sure they knew that I was ok, or at least, going to be ok.

That night in the hospital was one of the very few times throughout my entire cancer journey, that I was sad, truly sad. I was saddened by the fact that I had lost a part of my body that made me feel feminine, even though I knew it was the right thing to do to save my life. The saddest part was when the nurse wanted to check my incisions. I was sitting on the edge of the bed as she unwound the gauze that was covering my incisions. When all of the bandages were off and without being prepared for what I was going to see, I looked down at where my breasts used to be and I almost gasped. The nurse never asked if I was ready to see myself and didn't have any comforting words for me once she saw my reaction at the sight of my deformed chest. I didn't want to look but I couldn't take my eyes off of my concave chest and the two 5-inch incisions that ran horizontally across where my breasts had been taken. I imagined that when my breasts were removed, I wouldn't look much different than before because I had small breasts, but I would never had imagined the sight I was looking at. I couldn't even speak because I was so stunned.

The nurse tightly wrapped me up again and I lay in bed for the rest of the night alone and sad. Nobody could have made me feel any better if they were there with me. I just needed to be alone to process the day's events. I went home the next day and spent a few more days in bed. My sadness lingered on.

I didn't want to see anyone and I really didn't want anyone to see me. I had no hair on my head, no eyebrows, no eyelashes, and now, no breasts. I wanted to take a few days off from being "on" as I had been throughout most of my journey. I didn't even want to talk with anyone. I just wanted to be sad and grieve my loss. A part of my body had just been taken from me and I felt less than a whole person.

The Footprints Poem

One night I dreamed a dream.
As I was walking along the beach with my Lord.
Across the dark sky flashed scenes from my life.
For each scene, I noticed two sets of footprints in the sand,
One belonging to me and one to my Lord.

After the last scene of my life flashed before me,
I looked back at the footprints in the sand.
I noticed that at many times along the path of my life,
especially at the very lowest and saddest times,
there was only one set of footprints.

This really troubled me, so I asked the Lord about it.
"Lord, you said once I decided to follow you,
You'd walk with me all the way.
But I noticed that during the saddest and most troublesome
*   times of my life,*

there was only one set of footprints.
I don't understand why, when I needed You the most, You
   would leave me."

He whispered, "My precious child, I love you and will never
   leave you
Never, ever, during your trials and testings.
When you saw only one set of footprints,
It was then that I carried you." —Mary Stevenson

I had heard of this poem but it didn't resonate with me until I had cancer. I didn't put myself at the end of my life looking back; I just focused on the one set of footprints, totally believing that Jesus was carrying me through the tough times in my desert.

The suffering I endured through this was not only physical and emotional, but also spiritual. I wasn't spending much time with Our Lord, outside of church, and, although, I said that I felt instant trust in God, I didn't have a relationship with Him where I could go to Him at any time and know that He was there for me.

Part of my sadness and loneliness was also *not* knowing, or believing or even thinking that God was with me in my hospital room. I didn't blame Jesus, I wasn't even mad at Him. I thought nothing of Him. Total void of His Presence. I know now that He *was* there and He *was* walking me through the desert so I would find Him and follow Him.

Then Jesus was led up by the Spirit into the wilderness to be tempted by the devil. He fasted forty days and forty nights, and afterwards he was famished. The tempter came and said to him, "If you are the Son of God, command these stones to become loaves of bread." But he answered, "It is written,

   'One does not live by bread alone,
     but by every word that comes from the mouth of God.'"

Then the devil took him to the holy city and placed him on the pinnacle of the temple, saying to him, "If you are the Son of God, throw yourself down; for it is written,

> *'He will command his angels concerning you,'*
> *and 'On their hands they will bear you up,*
> *so that you will not dash your foot against a stone.'"*

Jesus said to him, "Again it is written, 'Do not put the Lord your God to the test.'"

Again, the devil took him to a very high mountain and showed him all the kingdoms of the world and their splendor; and he said to him, "All these I will give you, if you will fall down and worship me." Jesus said to him, "Away with you, Satan! for it is written,

> *'Worship the Lord your God,*
> *and serve only him.'"*

Then the devil left him, and suddenly angels came and waited on him. (Matthew 4:1-11)

When Jesus spent 40 days in the desert, He was preparing for his ministry and ultimately, His death. He was tempted by the devil but did not give in. Although, I don't remember feeling tempted by the devil during my walk through the desert, I believe that the devil was winning the battle by keeping me away from Jesus and not seeking Him out for comfort.

I so wish I would have been able to find comfort in knowing Jesus was with me during those days after my surgery. I wonder how I would have felt if I had the relationship I have now with Him, then. Would it have taken some of the sadness away? Yes. I think I would have still felt sad, but my time in the desert would not have been so long.

Even though I walk through the valley of
the shadow of death, I fear no evil.

PSALM 23:4

Potholes Along the Way

AFTER HEALING FROM MY SURGERY, I met with my oncologist again to discuss my next treatment plan. My new chemo was called Taxol, and the side effects of that drug was more bone pain than nausea. I had four treatments every other week for eight weeks, just like my first go round.

The prediction of having bone pain was spot on. I think I had one of the worst nights in my life after having my first round of Taxol. It was even worse than delivering my three daughters without epidurals! The pain in my legs and pelvis were excruciating and the ibuprofen I took didn't seem to touch the pain. I slept for about two hours, then woke up moaning and groaning, and wanting to scream. Finally, around 5:30 in the morning, I lost it. I was crying and had to wake Val up, asking him to massage my legs. I know he felt so helpless all night not knowing how to relieve my pain. He asked if we should go to the ER and I kept telling him no because I thought that I could handle it. I was wrong. I couldn't tell if massaging my legs helped or not, but I finally fell asleep while Val was massaging them for about an hour more. I called the doctor's office as soon as it opened and was told to take my prescription for pain. I was trying not to take the prescription pain meds because it had gotten me sick when I had taken it before.

The lesson I learned that night? Not to dismiss any pain or think that my pain wasn't worth seeking help, even in the middle of the night. I always encourage others to have their health concerns checked out. Not only does it give them peace of mind but it also gives the doctors a heads up to know if their concern is significant or not. From that point on, I chose to make a trip to the Emergency Room, at any time of the day or night.

Saint John Paul II showed us how suffering can be used for the good of others. He endured not only old age but also Parkinson's disease. He believed that growing old was simply a biological process that everyone naturally goes through and along with it is some sort of suffering. By accepting God's plan for us, we can turn our suffering into a grace. I'm sure this saint offered up his suffering for many souls. I didn't know the term, "redemptive suffering" or when people said, "Offer up your suffering" until I experienced great suffering myself. When we suffer, we can make something good come of it by praying for others who may be suffering. I first heard about offering up my suffering for the lonely souls in Purgatory. They cannot pray for themselves so they need us to pray for them.

Everyone will endure pain and suffering some time in their lives. It's what we do with that suffering that will make a difference in how we view suffering.

I pour out my complaints before God
and tell him all my troubles.

PSALM 142:2 – 3

At Your Service!

Jesus, knowing that the Father had given all things into his hands, and that he had come from God and was going to God, got up from the table, took off his outer robe, and tied a towel around himself. Then he poured water into a basin and began to wash the disciples' feet and to wipe them with the towel that was tied around him. He came to Simon Peter, who said to him, "Lord, are you going to wash my feet?" Jesus answered, "You do not know now what I am doing, but later you will understand." Peter said to him, "You will never wash my feet." Jesus answered, "Unless I wash you, you have no share with me." Simon Peter said to him, "Lord, not my feet only but also my hands and my head!" Jesus said to him, "One who has bathed does not need to wash, except for the feet, but is entirely clean. And you are clean, though not all of you." For he knew who was to betray him; for this reason he said, "Not all of you are clean."

After he had washed their feet, had put on his robe, and had returned to the table, he said to them, "Do you know what I have

done to you? You call me Teacher and Lord—and you are right,
for that is what I am. So if I, your Lord and Teacher, have washed
your feet, you also ought to wash one another's feet. For I have
set you an example, that you also should do as I have done to
you." (John 13:3-15)

T HE FIRST HOLY THURSDAY MASS that I can remember
going to was when I was living in Florida. It made
quite an impact on me. It's actually what brought me
back to Church. Throughout the years, though, I had been
attending Holy Thursday Mass sporadically. As I was finishing up my year of cancer treatment, Sally and I were asked
if we would like to have our feet washed on Holy Thursday.
It has been the tradition at our parish to have the leaders of
our church wash the feet of twelve people, representing the
apostles, who have had a cross to bear in one way or another
during the past year.

Sally thought it was neat that we were going to have our feet
washed but when she realized that it was going to be in front of
the entire congregation, she wasn't so sure she wanted to do it.
I told her it would be fine because everyone there loved us so
much. When it was time, Sally and I walked up holding hands
and sat down on the chairs that were placed on the perdella. I
had asked God to help me stay composed and He answered my
prayer. I didn't cry. Our pastor washed my feet first. The water
was very warm and his touch was gentle. I tried to imagine
Jesus washing my feet telling me, "What I am doing, you do not
understand now, but you will understand later." Sally was next
and she sat up a little taller in her chair, her little feet dangling
even farther away from the floor. I smiled as I watched Father
Tom wash her feet. I wondered what was going on in her little
5 year old mind and I know she didn't understand what the feet
washing meant. We walked hand in hand back to our pew and

Sally looked up at me with a big smile on her face. That just about brought me to tears!

Now I really look forward to Mass on Holy Thursday each year. It puts me at the Last Supper with Jesus as He takes off his outer garment and bends down to wash the feet of His Apostles. What a profound example of humility for the Messiah to wash the parts of the body that were undoubtedly, the most abused, calloused and probably deformed from use at that time in history. Jesus loves us so much and He shows that by caring for our every need and goes so far as to giving up His life for us. We are called to be like the twelve apostles and to allow Jesus to model for us, what we are called to do, to serve others. We are called to be like Jesus and show love for others unconditionally.

It is also our responsibility to receive love and care with grace and humility. Throughout my journey and especially at the very beginning of it, our family received much care. We had meals delivered to us and had a housecleaning service paid for by our community. At first, it was difficult to accept these wonderful and gracious gifts. We thought we could do it on our own, and we probably could have. But we didn't need to. We just needed to be thankful and grateful for the support. I have learned that it is a wonderful gift to those who love us and want to help us, to receive their help with grace and joy.

At that particular Holy Thursday, I appreciated the opportunity for Sally to represent my family who also suffered through my cancer. They had their own version of my cross to carry. Even though their suffering may not have been as physical as mine, they still suffered in their own way. It was an experience that will always remain close to my heart.

Just as Jesus told His apostles, I did not understand fully what I was suppose to do with this cross I was given, but as I continue to grow in my faith, my understanding of my cross becomes clearer each day. I can recognize the opportunities that I am given to wash the feet of others, to serve them with love and mercy and humility. Sharing my journey with you has been one way that I am serving God.

Walk worthy of the calling with which you were
called, with all lowliness and gentleness.

EPHESIANS 4:1

Under (Re)Construction

VAL AND I HAD AN APPOINTMENT with a plastic surgeon to discuss my breast reconstruction options, and we liked her very much. We chose the option of having tissue expanders, because it was the least invasive surgery. Tissue expanders are exactly what they sound like; they stretch the skin in the breast area for implants to be placed to reconstruct breasts. During my surgery to place my tissue expanders, I was given an injection of Botox to help with some of the pain that is expected, as my skin is stretched. Botox "paralyzes" the muscles and may last up to three months. I began having fills immediately. Fills are amounts of saline that is used to stretch the expander. As a matter of fact, my surgeon gave me my first injection of saline while I was still in surgery.

The normal time between fills may be every seven to ten days, but because I didn't understand the whole process of reconstructive surgery, I had no idea how much time it took. My doctor wanted me to begin radiation by the first week in January 2008, so I had my tissue expanders placed the day after Thanksgiving and had saline fills every five days after that. I needed to get to the size I wanted my breasts to be before I began radiation because once my skin was radiated, it wouldn't stretch as well.

I expected to be in pain from the surgery but wasn't prepared for what I got. After a few days of not being able to do much of anything but lay in bed, on propped up pillows, with my arms by my sides. I was able to shower, washing my hair with one hand at a time. The muscles in my arms hurt, too, causing me not to be able to lift my hands over my head. I wasn't able to open my medicine bottles, but I was able to sleep pretty well, thankfully, but there was a lot of pain as my skin was stretched more and more by the end of the day of a fill. I wouldn't be able to lift my arms because of the pain. I remember driving home from a fill and having to hold the steering wheel at the bottom because it hurt too much to hold it any other way. Hailey had to even feed me dinner once. I had a heating pad on my upper back and my chest and it helped with the pain, though, I had to sleep propped up for several weeks and then flat on my back even longer. Eventually, the pain subsided and life was good! I remember having a conversation with my plastic surgeon as she was examining my skin that was stretching over the tissue expanders. "Rhonda, you have thin skin." I told her that may be true in the physical sense of the words, but it was NOT true in the proverbial sense!

I needed to keep the tissue expanders in for six months in order for a 'pocket' to be formed where my breast implant would be placed, similar to when someone has braces on their teeth, they get to where the teeth are straight and beautiful but the braces need to stay on the teeth for a couple more months to ensure that they won't move once the braces are taken off.

Sally asked me one day what the tissue expanders looked like. Because she was only five years old, I had to explain to her as simply as I could so she would understand. I told her that they were like water balloons and each time I saw the doctor, she would put more water in them to make the balloons stretch.

"How does the doctor put the water in?" Sally asked.

"With the needle," I said.

"Won't the needle pop the water balloon?" She replied. What a smart little girl! I explained that there was a small port in the water balloon that the doctor could put the water in and it wouldn't pop the balloon. But that didn't stop her questions.

"What color are the balloons, red or pink or yellow?" She wondered.

"No, honey, just plain white," I said with a smile on my face and in my heart.

Just as Sally approached my cancer journey with her child-like perspective, totally trusting me when I explained things to her and told her that I was going to get better, without realizing it, I also approached my journey with a childlike perspective. My faith was in its infant stage and I believe that is why I had total trust from the very beginning that God would take care of me. It was such a blessing to have that point of view and it gave sweet pleasure to Jesus.

After, almost exactly one year (six days shy) of my diagnosis, I finally had my last surgery for my breast reconstruction. The plan was to have my port removed, have a laparoscopic hysterectomy, and replace my tissue expanders with silicone implants all in one surgery, using two different surgeons. I was very happy for that day to arrive, but I wasn't sure about how I was going to feel after that surgery.

Just as I expected my body hurt from head to toe, well, actually from neck to knees. I had one small incision in the removal of my port, two large incisions across my breasts and four small ones for my hysterectomy. The incisions on my breasts were open and closed, three times in the past year. Those poor things.

I have read in the bible many times that my body is a temple and that I should treat it like one. I used to think that meant that I should eat right and exercise. Yes, that's part of taking care of my temple but more importantly; I need to nourish my soul with God's word and His spirit, in order to keep my temple strong in case of adversity.

The several years leading up to being diagnosed, I was in the best physical condition that I had been since college softball days, probably even better. Some would wonder how cancer can find its way into a healthy body and would be disappointed at the reality that cancer does not discriminate. I was fortunate to be in good health when I was diagnosed because it helped me heal from surgeries quickly and rather smoothly and I really feel that I was able to handle the chemo better because my temple was strong.

The more important lesson here is that my faith has been the "cornerstone" or the "building block" that my temple was built on and without it, I really don't know, or want to know, where I would be.

My temple has been bruised and beaten with chemo, scarred by surgeries and procedures, and yet, it is still perfect in the eyes of God. The heart of my temple, though hurt and weak at times, has been strong and continues to endure whatever God's plan is for me.

Cancer will not destroy my temple.

*Do you not know that you are a temple of God
and that the Spirit of God dwells in you?*

1 Corinthians 3:16

Light at the End of the Tunnel

FTER A YEAR OF DOCTOR'S APPOINTMENTS, scans, and surgeries, I could see the light at the end of the tunnel and I was really looking forward to moving on to my new "normal" life. I was a changed woman, both physically and spiritually, and I couldn't wait to see in which direction God was going to lead me. My body had been fine tuned and my spiritual gas tank was full.

My medical routine was to see my oncologist every three months for the first year or so, then every six months for a couple of years, and finally, seeing her once a year indefinitely. The goal for any breast cancer survivor is to make it to that golden five year mark because the chances of recurrence drop pretty dramatically after five years. But, again, I needed to trust in God's plan, not the medical community.

So, I was just coasting along the path of life…then Val and I received an invitation from our oldest daughter, Ashley. She was a freshman in high school and was attending her first Quest retreat. Quest retreats are for confirmation candidates and it's a weekend of sacraments, prayer, and growing toward the Lord.

I attended my first mom's retreat at St. Michael's. This retreat, along with a dad's retreat, were created for the parents of our confirmation candidates to get a taste of what the freshmen experienced at their first Quest retreat. The kids would experience some amazing moments and would go home to tell their parents about it and some parents wouldn't be able to relate to their child because they, themselves hadn't experienced anything like their child did.

At one point in the weekend, everyone has the opportunity to write a letter to someone and when Ashley was a freshman, she wrote a letter to Val and me. In it, she shared how the weekend was going, how her desire to grow in her faith was growing, and she asked us to attend our corresponding weekends that were coming up. She invited us to attend the Parent retreat that would mimic what her weekend was like, so we would have an idea of the experience she had.

Of course, we wanted to support our daughter in her excitement of her budding faith, so we signed up for the retreat and what happened at that retreat opened the door even wider for my faith to grow by leaps and bounds! My cancer diagnosis opened my eyes and heart to the Lord and His goodness, but this retreat put Val and me on a road to great devotion to preparing not only ourselves for heaven, but our three daughters. We accelerated slowly at first, test driving the abundant opportunities for us to grow our faith, and soon, we were cruising along, wanting to learn more and more about our faith.

This is the letter I wrote to Ashley during my weekend retreat:

Dear Sweetheart,

I am sitting in church, and I've just received the sacrament of reconciliation. I have to be honest, I've always been apprehensive to go to confession, I think, because I've been embarrassed to admit my sins. I know, and now believe, that God is forgiving and loves me, as imperfect as I am.

I'm glad I am experiencing this weekend like you did last weekend. I love you very much and I'm very proud of you, and I'm excited to share with you, your faith journey. You have a great foundation and through the next two years, you are going to be blown away with experiences and you are going to have God, by your side, every step of the way.

I want to have a better relationship with Jesus and Mary. I'm hoping that you and I can share our thoughts and feelings with each other and grow together. With dad going next weekend, the three of us will have a connection that I hope will grow strong.

I love you very much!
Mom

As he walked by the Sea of Galilee, he saw two brothers, Simon, who is called Peter, and Andrew his brother, casting a net into the sea—for they were fishermen. And he said to them, "Follow me, and I will make you fish for people." Immediately they left their nets and followed him. As he went from there, he saw two other brothers, James son of Zebedee and his brother John, in the boat with their father Zebedee, mending their nets, and he called them. Immediately they left the boat and their father, and followed him. (Matthew 4:18-22)

Can you imagine what Simon and Peter must have thought when Jesus said to them to drop everything and that He would make them fishers of men? Or, when James and John up and left their father and never looked back? They may have been a bit overwhelmed or maybe they thought they were not qualified to do what he asked. Those were ordinary men but God saw something in them that they didn't. Not all of the Disciples traveled the world or wrote gospels but they all had something in common, their love for the Lord.

If we let the Holy Spirit lead us, we too, can proclaim the gospel to the people in our own little world around us. We don't need to travel far to reach the souls of many. Every encouraging word that we speak can bring others closers to Christ. Every act of kindness we perform shows the love that Jesus has for us. Every time we forgive, even in the smallest way, reflects the mercy Jesus shows us time after time.

So, don't disqualify yourself! Just pray to Jesus for whatever you need to reach others and show them His generous love. Ashley reached out to us with her invitation to follow her along her faith journey and we accepted it and we will forever be grateful for her doing that. Don't worry if you don't know what you need, because He does!

> *So that you may announce the praises of*
> *him who called you out of the darkness.*
>
> *1 Peter 2:9*

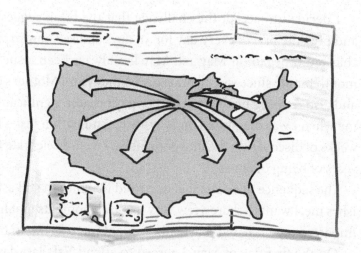

Expanding Your Territory

Jabez was more honorable than his brothers, and his mother named him Jabez saying, "Because I bore him with pain." Now Jabez called on the God of Israel, saying, "Oh that You would bless me indeed and enlarge my border, and that Your hand might be with me, and that You would keep me from harm that it may not pain me!" And God granted him what he requested. (Chronicles 4:10)

I WAS GIVEN MANY BOOKS when I was diagnosed with cancer. Some sat on my bookshelf for a while before I had any desire to read them. One in particular, *The Prayer of Jabez* caught my eye one day. Hailey had been talking about this book and within days, I saw it sitting on my bookshelf. It had sat there for almost five years without me even looking at it, but once I realized that God connected the book to both Hailey and I within days of each other, I knew I needed to read it. And, boy did it make an impact on me!

I decided to accept the challenge that the book suggested and pray the prayer every day for 30 days and see how my life changed. I began on May 1st. May has always been a special month for me since we celebrate my birthday and Mother's day, and also Ashley's birthday. Another day became significant to me when I was diagnosed on May 18th. And within just a few weeks of discovering the Prayer of Jabez, I would celebrate five years of being diagnosed!

The sequence of events that occurred that month still astonishes me. I want to share a few very integral moments that have impacted my faith and maybe they might interest you to try.

On the first day of May, I agreed to attend Val's last day of Bible study. He had been attending this Bible study and thought I would really like it. I hesitated but I decided to go. This was the first time I heard Jeff Cavins speak and I was hooked! After that, I joined Val and participated in several Bible studies with Jeff. I've learned so much from him and I will always be grateful for him sharing his wisdom.

On the fifth of May, I took my mom to see Matthew Kelly speak. I read his book, *Rediscover Catholicism*, a few years prior to this and it was the first book I read that was an integral part of my faith journey. I had listened to several CDs of Matthew Kelly but going to the event was such a great experience. I really felt that Matthew was speaking directly to me at times. I felt connected to what he was saying and it was neat when he would start telling a story that I'd heard before. It was even better when he added something new to the story that I could relate it to my life. I loved laughing with him and listening to his Australian accent.

I was amazed at all of the ways that I felt Jesus with me during that 30 day challenge. It really opened my eyes to be able to see how present He was in my life. It gave me great comfort and also inspired me to want to seek Him more and more. Val even noticed a change in me. I didn't stop praying the prayer because I was happy with the results for 30 days and I wanted to see what another month might do to my faith.

At that time in our lives, our oldest daughter, Ashley, was graduating from high school and would be going off to college in the fall. We decided to simplify our lives and sell our big house and move into a townhome. It was the first time I ever prayed a novena and it was to St. Joseph, the patron saint of families and households, for him to find the perfect family to buy our house. Val is a realtor and also a very faith-filled man. He prays for his clients and when their house goes on the market, Val will give them a statue of St. Joseph. Not to be buried, but to be honored in a special place in their home.

What a transformation I made in two months! The Prayer of Jabez had transformed me tremendously. It had shown me God's plan to sell the house and live on what we needed not what we wanted. I prayed for God to continue to guide us to do His will.

The Prayer of Jabez helped me to see God's handiwork in my faith life and it also empowered me to begin to expand my territory by sharing my faith with others. I encourage you to pray the prayer of Jabez for 30 days and see how God expands your territory! Be sure to jot down your thoughts during that time. I think you will be just as amazed as I was!

*Put out into deep water and
lower your nets for a catch.*

LUKE 5:4

Destination Reached!

I WAS SO EXCITED to celebrate the fifth anniversary of being diagnosed. Actually, I always considered myself a survivor the day I was diagnosed because my goal was to survive so that is the day I celebrate each year. I remember hearing that being five years out from diagnosis and remaining cancer free during that time is a good indication of remaining free for most people. I reached my destination!

I used my CaringBridge site to keep my family and friends updated with my health and activities and, of course, I had to share the following with everyone since it was a great time to celebrate:

May 18th, 2012
I can see the sun rising through the trees. Thank you for giving me
this beautiful sight this morning. The words you have engraved
on my heart are what have helped me get through this day 5

years ago. "Trust in Me"-"I will take care of you"-"I am with you always". Without knowing it, you were transforming me into becoming a better servant for You by having me experience breast cancer.

Please bless everyone who prayed for, cared for, and support-ed me in many other ways when I was going through my jour-ney. Please bless me that I remain cancer free and excited about helping others. Please help me be humble in my service to You.

We took the girls out of school for lunch at Applebee's to cel-ebrate the special day. I thought that gesture was very thought-ful but little did I know what else the family had planned for me. Val pulled out his iPhone and began to show me clips of each of the girls wishing me the best! Tears were welling up but Val was prepared, he pulled tissues out of his pocket. Then, Val's video played, and the tears spilled onto my cheeks as I heard his heartfelt words for me. I thought that was all of the videos but I was wrong. There were clips from some of my sisters, sis-ters-in-law, brother, and brothers-in-law! By this time, I could barely see through my tears. It was so awesome! Val said there were two more videos, but he thought we might want to wait on them because I was so emotional. I said we might as well continue since I was already a mess! The next video he showed me was from my mom. As soon as I saw her face, I began to full out cry. Her words were loving, but what struck me most was that she said she doesn't cry very much and as she was speaking the words she got very emotional, which made me cry even more! But, I have to say that the most moving video award goes to my dad. He was sitting on his lawn mower, with the lake as his backdrop. He began congratulating me on my anniversary and was sniffling and then . . . he told Val to stop the video! My tough dad turned into a big marshmallow! That just about put me away! By this time, I was using our napkins since all of the tissues had been used already! Val played the second video from dad and he said such wonderful things to me. Words that I know he has felt about me but I'm not sure he has verbalized them in the beautiful way that he did that day. I was so moved. I wasn't the only one at our table crying by this time! My day could have ended right there and it would have been the best day ever! But it didn't! Val pulled out a little black box with a beautiful cross necklace made with pink stones. It was perfect! Ashley put it on me as I was trying to compose myself. And, we hadn't even eaten yet! Another wonderful gift was Ashley offering to say grace. Her words just made me so proud to be her mom.

I received cards, phone calls, a many hugs from my friends and family. I have been truly blessed! Those five years had given me so many opportunities to be a good and faithful servant for God. He led me down many paths in order to help others. My life was fantastic! I followed Jesus and I found the light of healing. "I am the light of the world, if you follow me, you won't have to walk in darkness, because you will have the light that leads to life." (John 8:12)

The house that we lived in at that time had windows that faced east so I had a special chair with a small table next to it that hosted my prayer books. I am an early riser and my favorite time of the day was early morning, especially when I could watch the sun rise over the trees outside my window. Some mornings, the sky was pink, which I took as a special message from God, letting me know He was with me, and it would sometimes bring tears to my eyes. As my faith continued to deepen, I was able to recognize small moments like that and appreciate those blessings in my day.

As the sun continued to rise and would shine on my face, I felt the warmth of God's love and wanted to share that love with others. I wanted to be a light for those who were experiencing darkness in their lives. I asked God to let His light shine through me.

> *I will bring health and healing to it; I will heal my*
> *people and will let them enjoy abundant peace.*
>
> JEREMIAH 33:6

At a Crossroads

JUST A FEW MONTHS AFTER CELEBRATING my five year anniversary, Val had a mole removed from his arm. The doctor told him that she was concerned with the size of it and the depth she needed to go to remove the mole. When she got the pathology report, it confirmed that it was melanoma. Not knowing anything about melanoma, we were a little concerned. One morning, Val was pretty scared and upset by the possibilities and it was my first opportunity to be the caretaker instead of the patient. I knew how he felt and I think that helped calm his fears.

Val and I had an appointment to see the surgical oncologist. He talked with us a bit and then wanted to examine Val. The doctor left the room for just a few moments and when the doctor came back in and sat down, we were still thinking that everything was just fine. The doctor had a piece of blank paper and began writing numbers and abbreviations and soon I was hearing that Val would need to have more area taken around where the mole was to get clear margins. I understood that from my experience. The doctor took his green marker and measured and drew a line on the tricep of Val's right arm, where he thought he would have to take the skin and tissue for a clear margin. It was a sizable area. Val teased by asking if that would make him look tough. The answer was, "It's going to look like a shark bite." So, Val would have a funny looking scar, a thinner arm, we could live with that. Ok, let's do it.

The doctor went on to the next bullet point on his sheet of paper. He explained how he was going to test the nodes and then said something that I couldn't believe I heard correctly. I can't remember the exact words but it was something like, "if the lymph nodes are involved, we can only prolong his life at this point." WHAT? What did he just say? This isn't THAT serious! The doctor said more but I don't remember any of it.

The third bullet was treatment after surgery. A PET/CT scan was ordered to see if the cancer was anywhere else in Val's body. Again, this is standard procedure for those diagnosed with cancer. If there was, it was very serious. I was really having a difficult time comprehending what I was hearing. I asked the doctor how he felt about this and he said, "I don't like what I see and I want the PET scan to come back clear." When I had my first PET scan, I didn't realize how crucial it was for it to come back clear. I understood this time, though.

The doctor talked a bit more and he looked at his phone calendar and saw that he had an opening for surgery within just days. I couldn't believe that the doctor was scheduling his own surgery AND doing it so quickly! He left and the nurse came back in. She was hoping to have Val get his scan done right then!

Why such urgency? This was really scaring me. Finally, the PET scan was scheduled for Saturday morning and his surgery was set for Monday morning, just four days away. He needed to have a pre-op physical done that day. Another woman came in and talked with us but neither of us heard a thing. We both just wanted to get out of that room. We found our way back to our car and started for home—stunned and shocked.

All the way home, we would cry then compose ourselves, then cry again. Val said I was supposed to show him how to be tough, since I had been the one with cancer before. I told him that he needed to show me how to be the loving caregiver, since that was his role during my cancer. We spoke those words through our tears, half serious and half joking, but it was the truth. Our roles had been reversed. This experience was drastically different than mine.

Our minds were going a hundred miles an hour. When should we tell the girls? How should we tell the girls? When and how do we tell our family and friends? Things were happening so fast. Telling our loved ones was always such a difficult thing to do. To see the fear in their eyes was devastating at times. I dreaded it.

Amazingly, Val needed to go back to the office before coming home. Those moments of having to go about as if nothing had happened, have been blessings to us. If we didn't have these distractions, I can only imagine how desperate we may have felt.

And, just like the day when I was diagnosed 5 years ago, we went to Hailey's soccer game that night and nobody had any idea what our day was like, including the girls.

Enter by the narrow gate. For the gate is wide and the way is easy that leads to destruction, and those who enter by it are many. For the gate is narrow and the way is hard that leads to life, and those who find it are few. (Matthew 7:13-14)

People have said to me that we didn't deserve to have to go through another cancer after what I had gone through with mine. Some were even mad and have said the words, "It's not fair!" We are not guaranteed a problem-free life. Nobody is. We were at a crossroads, we could have agreed with those who thought that our situation wasn't fair or we could take the "high road" and trust in God's plan for us. With our faith continuing to grow, we were beginning to understand our purpose here on earth and that was to show our faith in God's plan and to share our faith with others, hopefully, bringing them closer to God. With that same faith, processing what we heard that day was very scary, but we were still able to choose the narrow gate and trust in God's mercy for us. Our hope is to follow the path that leads to eternity, free of problems, in heaven with Jesus.

By waiting and by calm you shall be saved, in
quiet and in trust shall be your strength.

Isaiah 30:15

Check Engine Light!

Make friends with the problems in your life. Though many things feel random and wrong, remember that I am sovereign over everything. I can fit everything into a pattern for good, but only to the extent that you trust Me. Every problem can teach you something, transforming you little by little into the masterpiece I created you to be. The very same problem can become a stumbling block over which you fall, if you react with distrust and defiance. The choice is up to you, and you will have to choose many times each day whether to trust Me or defy Me.

The best way to befriend your problems is to thank Me for them. This simple act opens your mind to the possibilities of benefits flowing from your difficulties. You can even give persistent problems nicknames, helping you to approach them with familiarity rather than with dread. The next step is to introduce them to Me, enabling Me to embrace them in My loving Presence. I will not necessarily remove your problems, but My wisdom is sufficient to bring good out of every one of them. (Jesus Calling, HarperCollins Christian Publishers.)

I read this in my *Jesus Calling* devotional and I think it sounded silly at first, but if we can accept our situations and trust that God is preparing us for His great plan for us, we can look at our problems differently. And if we can trust Him, knowing He is creating a better person in us, we can, and should thank Him for it. This act of gratitude changes our whole way of looking at life.

The first problem that came to my mind was my ongoing stomach issue. No, it wasn't my cancer. I had beaten that and didn't plan on that ever being an issue again. I totally trusted that God's plan for me was going to be amazing, and the journey so far was proving just that. *Jesus Calling* suggested that I give my problem a name. I decided to name it GG, for Gurgle Gal. Not Giggle Gal, even though I love to laugh. GG it is! You have to say it with a French accent to make my friend sound really cool!

GG and I have become good friends over the past few years. We have play dates almost every day! She usually comes to my house to play, but sometimes, she surprises me when I am out and about and I'm not very happy with her when she does that. Sometimes she doesn't like what we have for lunch and I hear all about. We talk to each other a lot, but there are times when I can't understand what she is saying. She mumbles often and grumbles a lot! Often, I get a bit frustrated with GG and I ask her to leave, even plead with her to, which she does, eventually. As much as I'm thankful for our friendship, I wouldn't miss GG if she moved away.

I had hoped that GG would be a short-term friend, but as it turns out, she may be my friend for life, it seems. I had a procedure called, a "Pillcam", where I had to swallow a tiny camera which took thousands of pictures throughout my entire digestive system. The results showed a pinpoint ulcer, but otherwise, everything looked normal and no further treatment was necessary. What? Hello? Normal? I don't think so. As thankful as I was that nothing serious was found, I was still very upset that there was no identification of the pain and discomfort I had been experiencing for such a long time and that there was nothing that could be done to give me any relief.

So many emotions went through my mind and it was hard to decipher why I was feeling some of them. I felt immense relief that there was no new cancer. I felt anger, frustration, and thankfulness. I also felt ungrateful for feeling mad that they couldn't find anything. Embarrassed that I had been living with this for almost 3 years and it was "nothing." How many others were living with this and not sharing that drama with the world? I felt like never talking about it again. (That didn't last long).

It was right before 3:00 in the afternoon when the nurse called to tell me the findings of the Pillcam and I had gone into my bedroom to lie down on my bed to pray the Divine Mercy Chaplet. Tears began to trickle down my cheeks onto my pillow as I prayed the chaplet. Relevant Radio's host for the Chaplet is Drew Mariani and callers ask for special prayers for whatever is troubling them in their lives. That day, Drew told his listeners that at Mass that day he prayed for anyone who had to carry a cross for their whole lives. I guess that was me. I asked God what He wanted me to do with my stomach pain. I lay there and waited for His answer. He answered me with peace, the peace I find in the Chaplet and my trust in Jesus. The peace that I find in accepting whatever is placed before me, including my BFF, GG!

The "hour of power" that Drew calls the Divine Mercy Chaplet gave me pause to check my engine, in other words, to check my heart to remember my purpose here on earth. It is to serve God with all my heart and soul. To accept whatever His plan is for me and at this point, I was also called to serve Val as he began traveling on his own journey with cancer.

Consider it all joy.

JAMES 1:2

Rugged Road

Just then a lawyer stood up to test Jesus. "Teacher," he said, "what must I do to inherit eternal life?" He said to him, "What is written in the law? What do you read there?" He answered, "You shall love the Lord your God with all your heart, and with all your soul, and with all your strength, and with all your mind; and your neighbor as yourself." And he said to him, "You have given the right answer; do this, and you will live."

But wanting to justify himself, he asked Jesus, "And who is my neighbor?" Jesus replied, "A man was going down from Jerusalem to Jericho, and fell into the hands of robbers, who stripped him, beat him, and went away, leaving him half dead. Now by chance a priest was going down that road; and when he saw him, he passed by on the other side. So likewise a Levite, when he came to the place and saw him, passed by on the other side. But a Samaritan while traveling came near him; and when he saw him, he was moved with pity. He went to him

and bandaged his wounds, having poured oil and wine on them.
Then he put him on his own animal, brought him to an inn, and
took care of him. The next day he took out two denarii, gave them
to the innkeeper, and said, 'Take care of him; and when I come
back, I will repay you whatever more you spend.' Which of these
three, do you think, was a neighbor to the man who fell into the
hands of the robbers?" He said, "The one who showed him mercy."
Jesus said to him, "Go and do likewise." (Luke 10:25-37)

We decided that we would tell the girls about Val's surgery at
the end of the school week. We would get the girls off to school
and go to first Friday mass. Father Tom's homily spoke right
to me. He talked about how we can't pick and choose when we
are faithful; we need to live faithfully all of the time. I had been
doing a pretty good job at that, I think, but since Val's diagnosis,
Satan had come into my heart and tried to scare me. I needed
to continue to pray, "Jesus, I trust in You. Jesus, I trust in You.
Jesus, I trust in You."

We planned on going up to University of St. Thomas to tell
Ashley in person. It was the first week of Ashley's freshman year
at the UST and we were so thankful that we were able to drive
to campus to tell her in person. As we walked toward Ashley's
dorm, I took Val's hand and asked the Holy Spirit to be with
us and give us the words that Ashley needed to hear to not be
afraid. We had no idea if Ashley would be in her dorm room
but we thought that was the best place to start. Ashley's roommate met us as she was heading down the steps and told us that
Ash would probably be at lunch. We headed out the door and
Jack, my nephew, was standing there. It was the first time we
had seen him on campus. We talked with him for a little while
but didn't tell him anything because we wanted Ashley to hear
the news first. We were anxious to find Ashley so, we headed
to the Student Center.

On our way to the student center, we met Father Michael Becker, the Rector of St. John Vianney Seminary on the campus of St. Thomas. How amazing is God to put us exactly where we needed to be to see Ashley's roommate, Jack and Fr. Becker! Val told him why we were there and he immediately put his hand on Val's right shoulder and prayed over him. He blessed Val and said he would continue to pray for him. Val thought it was no coincidence that Fr Becker put his hand on the shoulder of the arm where his cancer was. Both Val and I were glad we had our sunglasses on because we had tears in our eyes after that special moment with Fr. Becker.

We tried calling Ashley earlier but didn't want to leave a voicemail message. Then, Val decided to text her, asking her to call him because we were on campus and had something important to tell her. She called us back right as we got to the student center plaza. Val tried to tell her to meet us there but once he heard Ashley's voice, he couldn't speak, which I'm sure scared Ashley, but he got the message out. I happened to turn around and I saw Ashley across campus coming our way. As soon as she saw us, she began running toward us and I could see the fear on her face. Just as she reached us, she began to cry a bit, she thought the news was about my cancer coming back. I took her hand and we went to sit at a table off to the side to have a little more privacy. Val and I took Ashley's hands and Val began to tell her Val's news. He only got out a few words before breaking down. The Holy Spirit kept me calm and I was able to tell Ashley everything we knew. She cried, Val cried and the three of us held each other's hands tightly. She had questions, of course, and we answered them as best we could. Soon, we were talking about school and how hard her classes were and that she signed up for swing dance lessons and intramural soccer! We were all laughing by the time it was for us to leave. We asked if she was going to be ok and she said that she was meeting friends for lunch and they would take care of her. This certainly wasn't the way any of us expected her first days of college to be like, but it turned out to be not so bad.

Val and I walked hand in hand back to our car, feeling much better than we did an hour before. We weren't in the car for more than a few minutes when we received a text from Ash, telling Val that she loved him. So, we were crying again, but this time, they were thankful tears.

We were going to tell Hailey and Sally after dinner that night and towards the end of the meal, he explained to the girls what we knew, I watched their faces to try to read how they were taking it. I was really surprised that Sally didn't look sad or scared. Now, being 10 years old, Sally was still young enough to not fully understand the seriousness of the situation. I don't even think she had tears in her eyes. I think her first words were, "Does that mean we're going to write another book?" *Mommy's Hats* was written shortly after my journey with cancer, so it may seem natural for her to think we would write another book. Hailey, on the other hand, looked more upset but she didn't have much to say or ask. She was just trying to keep it together. After several minutes, she excused herself and went to her room. She had been on this rugged road before and I'm sure memories of my journey came racing back to her mind. With Hailey being five years older since I went through my treatment, she understood more about cancer and what changes might take place in our lives.

God placed three people in our path that day. The first two did not treat us poorly or ignore us, but it was definitely the third traveler, the Good Samaritan who stopped and prayed over Val, gave us exactly what we needed and offered two silver coins in the form of continued prayers for our needs.

When you take the time to care for someone, not only does that person benefit from your love. You are being Christ-like and you, too, are receiving blessings from God when you offer kindness to your neighbor.

Have you been able to identify certain people, YOUR good Samaritans that God has placed in your path, exactly when you needed them? They may have been the checkout lady at the grocery store, complimenting you on your outfit or a friend calling you out of the blue to invite you to play golf. Looking back, I had many good Samaritans strategically placed on my path. When I thought I could not travel this rugged road, they were there to put spiritual air in my tires so I was able to continue traveling on this journey.

You shall love your neighbor as yourself.

Luke 10:27

Traveling Companion

Dear Jesus,

Today's devotion from 'Jesus Calling' was about trusting in you. "Practice trusting me on your quiet days when nothing seems to be happening. Then when the storm comes, your trust in me will see you through."

It is very pertinent to our lives always, but especially now. I read it to Val and he asked if I wanted to hear what he wrote in his journal. He wrote that he feels the closest to you more than he ever has and he said that he has total trust in you! He accepts your will and will take every opportunity to share his faith with others. You are amazing! I just love when you do that! I do so trust in you and I will accept whatever you have planned for us. I asked that you prepare us to serve you with strong faith.

We've received texts, emails, prayers from family and friends. I know you answer all prayers. I wonder how you will answer our prayers.

I think trusting you is one of the biggest and best things I can do in order to get through each day. Yes, there are many, many more quiet days than those killer storms. I trust you with every fiber of my being. I know you have a great plan for me. I know you will always be with me. The moments when Satan tries to make me worry are growing less and less, yet when he succeeds; it is when I need you the most. I will be scared for moments, but then my heart tells me, you are near.

Today I will trust whatever you place before me. It should be a quiet day. Please help me remember your love for me and for Val.

Is it your will that the tumor has shrunk or better yet disappeared? I absolutely believe in miracles, and I would shout it from the rooftop if you perform that miracle! And, it wouldn't only be me shouting your praises! Val, the girls and our friends and families would all be shouting! (Journal entry before Val's surgery)

VAL HAD SURGERY to remove the entire mole from the back of his arm and the doctor wasn't kidding when he said it would look like a shark took a bite out of his arm. Val remained calm the entire time. I was amazed, but then again, I wasn't. His trust in Jesus was amazing! All of the prayers and blessings he had received were overwhelming. Val even wanted to make sure that the doctor was blessed before he went into surgery and asked if I would bless him if Val didn't have the opportunity to do so. I wanted to see Val as he began drifting off to sleep but they wheeled him away quickly after I gave him one more kiss and an, "I love you." As he was being wheeled down the hallway toward the OR, just as I promised, I put my hands in the air and I said, "God bless you all and take good care of my honey."

The doctor said the PET scan came back really good with the exception of a small spot on Val's esophagus. The doctor didn't seem too worried about it and said that when Val was all healed surgery, he would have an endoscopy to see what was down there.

"Trust me." How often do we read that in the bible? Jesus encourages us to trust him completely. Our priest talked about fear during one his homilies at Mass. He explained to us that if we let God's love for us be received, then there is no room for fear. "Do not fear, I am here." That sounds like what Underdog would say, "Do not fear, Underdog is here!" (Footnote: Underdog was a popular cartoon in the 1960's, and the namesake hero dog's repeated cry was "There's no need to fear, Underdog is here!")

There are not too many things that I fear, and I thank God for that. I know as we drew closer to Val surgery, Satan would try to scare me with things that could possibly go wrong. I wanted to work extra hard to not let those thoughts creep into my mind. I prayed to St. Pio to fill me with grace to accept whatever God have planned for Val in our family. I prayed for strength for Val and the girls and me, for whatever was on the road ahead of us.

My living Presence is your companion
each step of the way.

ISAIAH 26:4

Wandering in the Wilderness

Dear Jesus,

I read in my daily devotional this morning, "Receive My Peace." I continue to find peace in my daily life since I have developed my relationship with Jesus. I am able to let go of many small issues that used to bother me. Peace is a gift from You, if I want to receive it.

I know Val has total trust in you and so do I. I feel like I'm lying to you when I say that at times because I'm emotional. Do you believe me? We'll find out today the results of Val's biopsy. Please be with us as we hear what your plan is for us. Give us grace to handle it to be great examples of your love and compassion. Thank you for all you have given us as we travel on this journey. You have touched Val's heart in a way he never expected. I've seen another transformation in him. You have strengthened the bond between you and Val and he is going to share that with anyone and everyone he can. He will definitely be enlarging his territory.

AFTER VAL RECOVERED from the surgery that removed the mole on the back of his arm, he had an endoscopy which included biopsying his esophagus to determine what the spot on it was. The procedure wasn't bad but it took a few extra days to get the results of Val's biopsy. I was not pleased with the waiting. It felt like we were wandering the in the wilderness, not knowing which direction to walk. Would the results be that the spot on his esophagus was cancerous? What would that mean? It is very unfortunate for those waiting for possible life changing results to have to wait for, what seems like a lifetime to some, the news. Val said that he was ok, whatever the results were. His faith was that strong. He was at peace with the results, even the waiting! I was accepting of God's plan as well, but I was still impatient as I waited to hear the final word. At that time I needed to find more peace and patience than I had. Blessed again, the results were good for the most part, with the exception of that small tumor on Val's esophagus.

> *Wait patiently with me while I bless you. Don't rush into My Presence with time-consciousness gnawing at your mind. I dwell in timelessness: I am, I was, I will always be. For you, time is a protection; you're a frail creature who can handle only twenty-four-hour segments of life. Time can also be a tyrant, ticking away relentlessly in your mind. Learn to master time, or it will be your master. I will bless you and keep you, making My face shine upon you graciously, giving you peace. (Jesus Calling)*

Take some time to sit quietly with Jesus and place your trust in Him regarding every aspect of your life. By doing this, you are able to release your problems and concerns to Him. You are able to sense peace. Be open to receive that peace, especially during the difficult days. This is when Jesus does His best work, if we let Him!

These troubles produce patience.

Romans 5:3-4

Tour Guide

J ANUARY 2013. A new year. A fresh start. A new beginning. I love the first day of the week, the month and especially, the first day of a new year. I always feel like making a change in my life, most of the time, it's a spiritual change. Now, I've tried many times to make a change in my life in order to make me a better servant for God. Many times, however, I have failed. And I will continue to fail, but I hope my efforts will not go unnoticed.

> For I know the plans I have for you plans to prosper you and not to harm you, plans to give you hope and a future. (Jeremiah 29:11)

This verse gives me peace because I trust that God wants the very best for me and I also trust that He has a lot for me to do here on earth before He calls me to heaven. I have come to really enjoy the quiet time early in the morning, when my mind is rested and the house is still. I enjoy hearing the clock tick at a rhythmic pace that accompanies my prayers. I enjoy sitting next to Val, glancing over at him as he reads, meditates and praises God.

As we continued to try to figure out what my stomach issues were, we found out that I needed to have my gallbladder removed and Val needed to have the tumor removed from his esophagus. My surgery was schedule at the beginning of the month and Val's was scheduled for the end of the month, to give me time to heal so I could take care of him. Knowing that this month would include surgery for both Val and I, we had additional prayers being said during those quiet times in the morning, and throughout the day, too. And yet, I was open to doing God's will and I was specifically asking for direction. I wanted God to speak to me, move me, and stir within me. I wanted to serve Him more. And, I wanted to feel His Presence at all times. I was craving Him immensely. I was still praying the prayer of Jabez, still wanting to be aware of the many blessings and opportunities that God was placing before me.

I wanted to know what God's plan was for me for 2013. What journey would He take me on? What road test would I have to take and hopefully pass? Whatever it was going to be, I had total confidence that God would be my Tour Guide the entire time. I knew He would lead me in the direction in which I needed to go and I knew He would equip me with whatever vehicle I need to drive to get there.

During another of Father's homilies, he talked about Simeon and Anna and how, of the hundreds of people in the temple with Mary and Joseph, as they presented Jesus, only those two were able to recognize Jesus as our Redeemer and Savior. They were righteous and devout and had a close personal relationship with God. Then, Father asked us if we looked around the church, would we be able to see Christ in the people that were sitting around us. Simeon and Anna had the grace and the understanding to be able to recognize the Savior of our world, unlike the hundreds of others that were there. Again, Father asked if we can see the face of Jesus in others that we see each day. Our challenge is to see beyond the obvious and the average, beyond the ordinary and the superficial. Father quoted Saint Teresa of Calcutta, "Dearest Lord, may I see you today and every day in the person of your sick, and whilst nursing them, minister unto you. Though you hide yourself behind the unattractive disguise of the irritable, the exacting, the unreasonable, may I still recognize you and say, 'Jesus, my patient, how sweet it is to serve you.'"

As I sat in my pew, I looked around the church and my eyes stopped on a couple of people. The first was a couple that was sitting directly in front of us. They were my in-laws; Loretta had her walker parked in the aisle and sat throughout most of Mass. My first vision of Christ was in her. Even though she may be in pain and may struggle to get to Mass, she was there. She was there because she wanted to celebrate and receive Jesus. When she was able to stand, my father-in-law would take her hand and hold it and even though I knew that their love for each other was very strong, he showed his love for his wife for the rest of the congregation to witness. It actually put a smile on my face when I saw him take her hand. My in-laws represent many in our church community who have been married for many years, who come to church, despite their pains and sufferings, and who know the joy in receiving Christ in the Holy Eucharist.

Then I saw a little baby, sitting on her mommy's lap with her tiny hands holding onto the back of the pew in front of her. She had her pacifier in her mouth and she was being such a good little girl throughout the entire Mass. She began tapping her hands on the pew and then, as soon as I fixed my eyes on her, she laid her head on her hands and her face was directly toward me. It was only for a few seconds but again, Jesus was looking right at me.

The memory of my friend, Dana, came to mind and I certainly saw the face of Jesus in her as I watched her take her last breaths. I saw Jesus in her as I stroked her cheek and told her that she didn't need to fight anymore. I continued to pray over her so that the last words she would hear were those of our heavenly Father and His Blessed Mother. Dana had suffered for the last several years with different health issues, but I very rarely heard her complain. Yes, she was ordinary on the exterior, maybe even a little rough around the edges, but she was certainly extraordinary on the inside. She was one of the first friends that I told of my diagnosis back in 2007 and she remained a dear friend until she received eternal peace.

My question for you is, can you see the face of Jesus in those you encounter each day? Can you imagine Him as your tour guide through life?

My safety and glory are with God,
my strong rock and refuge.

PSALM 62:8

Road Work Ahead

V AL WAS TOLD he needed to have the tumor on his esophagus removed. This would be major surgery because the tumor, as detected by the PET scan, was within the lining of his esophagus. This meant it would be very difficult to remove just the tumor without taking most of his esophagus and part of his stomach, which also meant possibly 10 days in the hospital, a feeding tube, and possibly unable to work for a couple of months. Ultimately, I knew Jesus, the Divine Physician would be with us and care for us.

This is the first email that I sent on the morning of his surgery:

7:22 AM, There was an emergency the surgeon needed to take care of so we are about two hours out yet. The hospital Catholic chaplain came and offered a beautiful blessing. Val has read his

89

readings for the day, said his prayers, prayed the Divine Mercy Chaplet and now he's resting (he's probably still praying).

The nurses had begun the process of preparing Val so we felt he was close to going into surgery. Val had wanted to bless the surgeon like he did for his first surgery, but he said if he was loopy, he wanted me to bless him. I instantly got tears in my eyes just thinking about that and wondered if I would be able to get any words out of my mouth. I asked him what he wanted me to say and he said, "Just 'God bless you and your staff,' and 'we have total trust in you.'" As we continued to wait, we were alone in the room. We held hands and looked at each other and our eyes filled with tears, each of us knowing what the other was thinking. We were scared. The only time Val ever mentioned the possibility of him dying from an unsuccessful surgery was when we thought the surgery was going to be in December, the original date that the surgery was set for. He said that was a big reason why he didn't want it then. He didn't want Christmas to be a reminder of his death. The doctor told him there was a 2% chance of the surgery being unsuccessful. It's a fact that had to be told, I knew that; as tiny of a percentage it was, there was always a chance to dying during any surgery. I believed it wouldn't happen but it was a thought that was difficult to put out of our minds. So when Val and I were looking at each other, there was just a hint of wonder if we would see each other again. I brought a tiny bottle of holy water that belonged to Sally and blessed Val with it, not only to bless him for the surgery but also just in case that would be the last blessing he received. I held his face in my hands and kissed him over and over.

Finally, the time came, and as Val was being wheeled down the hallway toward surgery, I raised my right hand and blessed the entire surgical team, and Val, and told them we had total trust in all of them. When they got to the end of the hallway and went through the last set of doors, I stood there for a few moments with peace in my heart, knowing that I was able to do what Val asked me to do. Then, it was all on the Divine Physician's hands and in the blessed hands of the highly skilled surgeon.

It was about an hour or so into the surgery that I realized I hadn't heard any update from the O.R., so I went to the info desk and asked if she could check the status of Val's surgery. I was hoping that the surgeon was able to determine whether or not Val needed the extensive surgery by that time, which is what he told us. Soon, a volunteer came to tell me that I had a phone call from the O.R. and I went to take the call at the information desk.

The O.R. nurse told me that the surgeon was able to take just the tumor! I had pictured myself receiving that wonderful news and also how I would react to the news if Val needed the long and invasive surgery. I thought of many dramatic scenarios, screaming, fainting, and crying in disbelief... I probably would have received an Oscar for my imaginary performances! As it was, I was quite calm as I received the news – the glorious news! I was told the surgeon still had some work to do but he would be finishing up the surgery soon. I thanked the woman on the other end of the phone, hung up and walked back to my waiting area, where my sister, Robin was. As I turned the corner and saw Robin, I blurted out, "They only had to take the tumor!" I burst into tears. Robin jumped off her chair and we were hugging each other and crying. I remembered telling friends that if Val only needed the tumor removed I would proclaim, "Praise the Lord!" And I did! I jumped up and down with my hands raised in the air saying, "Praise the Lord, Praise the Lord!"

I totally believe a miracle had just occurred.

The texts that were exchanged between our girls and I had so many exclamation points and capitalized words in them, you could just feel the unbelievable excitement and relief that we all felt! We had anticipated that the surgery would be extensive and didn't want to have the girls at the hospital all day. Ashley was home for J-term (having the month of January off) from college, so she was with Sally when she got home from school. Hailey was actually in Washington D.C. with the March for Life. I was very thankful that we were able to communicate with them, though.

As soon as I was composed enough I knew I needed to send out an email to share the wonderful news with our loved ones. Again, in all caps and lots of exclamation points, *'THEY GOT JUST THE TUMOR! PRAISE GOD! CAN YOU HEAR ME CHEERING FROM THE ROOFTOP? I CAN BARELY SEE THROUGH MY TEARS OF JOY!"*

It seemed like such a long time before I was able to see Val, even though it was only a couple more hours. I couldn't imagine how long it would have felt if he needed to have the extended surgery. As I walked around the corner on the floor that Val was taken to, there he was, being wheeled down the hall! I walked quickly, even ran a few steps to catch up with him. His bed was facing away from me so I walked up next to him and gave him two thumbs up. That was our sign that everything was great and it was only the "little" surgery. It was so good to see his face. I put my hands on his cheeks and kissed his forehead. I asked if he was in pain and his reply was, "I don't even care." He was so grateful for the simple surgery that he would gladly accept the pain that he was in.

"He looks great!" was on the subject line of the next email I sent out. 6:58 PM: You are all witnesses to a miracle today! Love you all!"

Then he took him by the right hand and helped him to stand up. Instantly his feet and ankles became firm, he jumped up, stood, and began to walk, and he went with them into the Temple, walking and jumping and praising God. Everyone could see him walking and praising God; and it is the name of Jesus which, through faith in him, has brought back the strength of this man whom you see here and who is well known to you. It is faith in him that has restored this man to health, as you can all see. (Acts 3:7-9, 16)

We've heard the story about the beggar that was crippled since birth. He would sit outside the "Beautiful Gate" and ask for anything he could get from the people who would be entering the Temple. A piece of food, a coin or two or some discarded clothing would be very welcoming for this man. But he received much more than he could have ever imagined from Peter and John. Peter said, "In the name of Jesus Christ the Nazorean, rise and walk." Peter, then, took the hand of the crippled man and the man stood up and was healed. He began praising God and all who were near, saw that he had been healed and were amazed.

The healing of this man was more than just physical healing; his hope had been restored in Jesus Christ. His whole life had changed in an instant and it was far more than he could have ever imagined. Our lives can change just like that, too, if we can turn to Jesus and ask Him to help us in any way that we need. I know that every person that is reading this has something to ask Jesus' help for. Ask for whatever it is that you need. When you do, be patient for His answer and be sure to thank Him for all the gifts He gives to you.

Our prayers were that Val would only need the shorter surgery and his strength would be restored. We also prayed for acceptance of God's plan for us and to restore our hope in His mercy and love. We never lost hope, but God certainly showed us that by going to Him with our needs and our praise, He can perform great miracles!

> *From the rising of the sun to its setting, the*
> *name of the Lord is to be praised!*
>
> PSALM 113:3

Another Traveling Companion

W HEN MY DAUGHTER, Hailey came home one day, and asked if we wanted to participate in a retreat called, "33 Days to Morning Glory", Val, Ashley and I accepted her invitation. Sally was a little too young to understand it, so she didn't do it. Ashley found it difficult to keep up with her job, so she decided to make the retreat another time. So, it was Val, Hailey and I. We chose to begin on June 13, 2013 which would make our consecration day July 16th, the feast of Our Lady of Mount Carmel. We chose these dates simply because it fit into our schedule the best. We were unaware at that time what God's plan was for us!

The retreat involves reading and studying the Marian devotion that four saints had; Saint Maximilian Kolbe, Saint Louis De Montfort, Saint John Paul II, and Saint Teresa of Calcutta.

Each shared why they loved our Blessed Mother so much and it gave me reason to love her as well. We studied each saint for a week, reading a few pages and reflecting on several questions each day. I highly encourage you to check it out and see if it is something you might be interested in. As we continued on the retreat, my relationship with our Blessed Mother grew deeper and my devotion to her became stronger. One example that sticks with me of how Mary intercedes for us to her Son is the image of me presenting Mary with an apple. Mary will take my simple apple; polish it up and place it on a beautiful golden platter, then gives it to her Son. The apple is my prayer as raw and ragged as they sometimes can be and she will make it beautiful as she asks Jesus to hear my prayer.

I know it can be difficult to understand the role that Mary plays in our lives, but even if you look at the absolute fact that Mary is the mother of Jesus, a role that took so much courage just to say "yes" to, it is clear that she would do anything for her Son, especially when it comes to bringing others closer to Him.

One of the amazing moments that we experienced during our retreat was the unexpected visit we made to the shrine of Saint Maximilian Kolbe in Marytown, Illinois. Hailey had a soccer tournament in Chicago and we realized we would be close to the shrine, so we checked it out. The shrine ended up being just minutes from our hotel! Val and I visited it while Hailey practiced and then the three of us visited it again when she had some free time. I had never heard of Maximilian Kolbe until the retreat, and there we were, at his shrine, learning more about his life and how he served God by serving others, and literally offering up his life for his neighbor.

Once I realized how important Mary's presence was in my life, I kept her close to my heart. I knew as soon as I finished the retreat that I was going to do it again the following year at the same time, which I did. I invited a small group of women from my Cursillo prayer group and we took turns hosting the weekly meetings at our homes. It was another wonderful experience. It was the same reading and the same questions, but I still learned a lot more about Mary and I saw her in a different light than I did just a year prior. I was in a different place in my life, as we all were.

My third year of consecrating, actually, it's considered re-consecrating myself to Mary, included almost 40 people from our parish that I invited to join me. This was very exciting to see the variety of people who wanted to consecrate themselves to the Blessed Mother. We learned so much from each other as we shared our experiences and thoughts about our readings. I love the idea of re-consecrating myself each year at the same time and I looked forward to seeing something new in my readings about those who had great devotion to Mary.

Since my consecration to Mary, I have been wearing a miraculous medal around my neck, almost constantly. It gives me something physical to touch when I need to be assured that Mary is with me, just as her Son is. I have prayed thousands of Hail Mary's at various times throughout the day. That prayer is so powerful! I love having Mary as another traveling companion. I can count on her at anytime and anywhere to help me through difficult moments.

When you look for me, you will find me.
JEREMIAH 29:13

Detour Ahead!

A S I READ, *Faith is the realization of what is hoped for, and evidence of things not seen.* (Hebrews 11:1) from *Jesus Calling* I stopped and read it again and again. I wanted to remember that line. Little did I know at that time that my faith would be tested later in the day.

Sally and I were out shopping for most the day, when we got home I received a phone call from a nurse at the cancer center. She told me that the results of my PET scan that I had earlier in the week came back and there was concern about some spots on my back that had changed from my scan several months ago. There were spots at that time, but the doctors were not concerned, yet now they became concerned because there were more spots, even though there weren't any places that "lit up" from the sugar water that was injected in me, which was a good thing.

So the nurse said that I need to have a bone marrow biopsy to give the doctors a better opportunity to know what was going on in my bones. Just the words, "bone marrow biopsy" made me cringe. My first thought was how painful it would be (from what I've seen on TV). I didn't even know if what I saw on TV was what I would be having done. Regardless, the nurse did say that it would be somewhat painful and said that I might feel like I was hit by a truck. Great.

I was offered the option of being sedated, I jumped at that option! The nurse was going to give me a lot of information and I had to ask her to give me a minute so I could gather my thoughts. I was just so surprised with the results that I was having a hard time comprehending what she was saying to me when I paused, the tears came. I didn't want to go there so I took a deep breath and prayed, "Mary, I need you! Please stay with me." Those words would not have come to my heart if I hadn't just completed the 33 Days to Morning Glory just TWO DAYS before that phone call! What a God moment! What a MARY moment!

Of course, my mind went into many directions, racing from one thought to the other. I wondered what Sally heard as I was speaking on the phone? If so, what was she thinking? I made a few exclamations during the phone conversation. Should I call Val or wait until he gets home? When should we tell the girls?

"Do not let your hearts be troubled. Believe in God, believe also in me. In my Father's house there are many dwelling places. If it were not so, would I have told you that I go to prepare a place for you? And if I go and prepare a place for you, I will come again and will take you to myself, so that where I am, there you may be also. And you know the way to the place where I am going." Thomas said to him, "Lord, we do not know where you are going. How can we know the way?" Jesus said to him, "I am the way, and the truth, and the life. No one comes to the Father except through me." (John 14:1-6)

It is very comforting to know that there is a special place just for me that Jesus has prepared for me. When I was younger, I pictured a room, like my bedroom, but cleaner! The walls were painted my favorite color and my bed was big and fluffy with lots and lots of pillows on it. It wasn't a perfectly clear picture in my mind. I think that was because of the mystery of heaven, so everything was a bit blurry.

I imagine every child has their own version of what heaven looks like and especially the place that Jesus has created for them. But, we don't have to wait until we go to heaven in order to be with Jesus. We have Him here with us wherever we are. He never leaves our side. We need to show Him that we trust Him by going to Him with our worries but not forgetting to go to Him in thanksgiving for what He has given us, each day.

While I was sitting with Jesus in Adoration earlier that week, I had my pen in my hand and my notebook open, waiting for Him to guide me to write what He wanted me to share with you. This is what I wrote: *Thy will be done, Surrender, Trust, Obedient.*

These are all words or phrases that generally mean the same thing. It is what Jesus wants us to do—Trust in Him, go to Him with our needs, follow Him, and allow Him to work in our lives. We can't let detours in our lives hold us back from living a life of joy.

Easier said than done, I know. But do we just give up and not even try to allow His plan to play out? Even for a day? I think you would be surprised at what happens when you "let go and let God." That was one of my favorite phrases during my first year of cancer treatment, just like "Thy will be done" continues to play in my head and heart.

Who's up for another challenge? Mission: Possible! Read the following words in the voice that spoke to Jim Phelps: (footnote: Jim Phelps was the special agent character in a popular spy series from the 1960s called "Mission Impossible." Each show began with a tape recording that Phelps would listen to before the secret tape would self-destruct.)

> *Good Morning, Child of God. Your mission, should you decide to accept it, is to spend a week, opening your heart to Jesus and trust what He wants you to do for Him. As always, should you be afraid or helpless, the Good Shepherd will NOT disavow any knowledge of your actions. This message will self-destruct in five seconds. Good luck, Child.*

I hope Jesus appreciated my silly sense of humor!

> *Unless you are faithful in small matters,*
> *you won't be faithful in large ones.*
>
> LUKE 16:10

Need a Tune Up?

JESUS TELLS US IN MANY DIFFERENT WAYS, that "nothing can separate you from My love." (Romans 8:35) and we must believe Him, especially when we are afraid or anxious. If we can just say the words we can find peace in our adverse circumstances. Our sadness comes when we feel unloved, when we feel betrayed. The feeling is usually worse than the actual situation, but with the assurance that Jesus is with us and loves us, we can feel safe and loved.

The long-awaited appointment with my oncologist had arrived and I wasn't concerned about being very emotional and I didn't expect to take very long. I was pretty sure I would have chemotherapy and I was also suspecting a port placed in my clavicle again, and I had no problem with that. Back in 2007, I dreaded just the thought of the port but once I had it and saw how much easier it was to administer my chemo through it. I realized it was blessing.

I'd been trying to guess the schedule of everything since I had become a seasoned vet. Normally, the doctors want treatment to begin right away and I was assuming that was going to be the case with me. I had a recent bone scan, which gave us the baseline of what condition my bones were in before I started chemo. The strong drugs could damage or weaken the bones. I had my labs drawn earlier in the week so that was taken care of. Obviously, I had a PET scan recently so I didn't need another one. Unless they want to see if a miracle had happened that removed the tumors in my back! I was ALWAYS open to a miracle!

In my, "been there, done that, so I know it all," mind, I could see me getting my port placed on Monday and chemo starting on Thursday. My oncologist has her patients have their chemo on Thursday since that's the only day that she is in the cancer center.

Val and I were quite pleasantly surprised at what my oncologist had to say. She explained that the reason that the PET scan and the blood tests didn't show any sign of cancer is because the cells are so tiny and less than 10% of my bones are involved. Praise God! My doctor's level of concern was low, which was very comforting to know.

My treatment would be two shots of **Faslodex** in my buttocks (that's their term but it is actually slightly higher in the hip than where I had my two biopsy samples taken). That drug was chosen because I was postmenopausal and because the cancer returned even though I had been taking tamoxifen. Faslodex is an anti-estrogen medicine similar to tamoxifen. I had them after my appointment with my doctor and went again every two weeks for the first two months. After that, I had the shots once a month for the next 9-12 months, depending on how well I was tolerating the drug and how effective it was. I would also have shot in my belly once a month, of **Denosumab**, to keep my bones strong.

There would be no port! No hair loss! No nausea! The most common side effect may be soreness or stiffness in the area of the injections. In other words, I could have (be) a pain in the butt! I asked my nurse, if she was going to have another nurse come in to give me the injections in my butt at the same time, just like they did when the girls were babies. She said no, I had to be a big girl. The Faslodex is thick and takes about a minute to inject. It was a long minute! I could feel the "stiffness" moving through my glute and down into my hamstring. Then, came the second injection...

The shot in my belly wasn't nearly as bad but still took a little longer than I thought it would. I set up the next several appointments and we were on our way!

I truly feel that our prayers have been answered. I kept my focus on Jesus and His path for me and He gave me peace in my heart. All I needed was a little spiritual tune up (prayer) and an oil change (new chemo) and I was ready to set out on the next stage of my journey.

A cheerful look brings joy to the heart and good news gives health to the bones.

Proverbs 15:30

Hills and Valleys

I HAD AN ENDOSCOPIC ULTRASOUND, as another procedure to determine what had been causing my stomach pain for the past two years. While the doctor was looking at my stomach, he wanted to take ultrasound images and tissue samples of the lining of my stomach. What the doctor found was that my stomach lining had become thick from the chemotherapy I received in 2007, which explained part of my stomach discomfort when I ate. I felt like I had a gastric bypass because my stomach felt very small, not allowing me to eat very much at all, resulting in losing almost 30 pounds. Because of the thickened lining, my stomach didn't stretch like it should when I ate, which made a lot of sense. I was happy to hear that my description was accurate. However, the doctor expressed his thoughts that breast cancer cells had found their way into my stomach lining.

I had decided that I was going to have this procedure done and one more at the end of the month, then, I was going to be done with trying to figure out what the deal was with my stomach pain. I had learned to live with the discomfort and pain for over two years. But, I thank God that I agreed to have that one last test done or else my prognosis may have been much worse. The Holy Spirit moved me to have that last test done, even though, I felt no answers would come from it.

On the way home, my mind continually went in many different directions, as it has each time I have received disturbing news. The devil was doing a good job putting dark thoughts into my head and distracting me from what I knew was true: that God's plan for me was a beautiful one and I just needed to stay focused on Him. I would tear up thinking about having to tell the girls, AGAIN, that the cancer had moved. I want them to know, but finding the right time was very difficult, and with Christmas being only days away. The girls had a couple days left of school before break with exams and celebrations. Ashley was lying on the couch when I got home and asked what we had found out and I made some comment like, "third time's a charm" or "here we go again". I wanted to make sure Ashley knew that everything was still going to be fine so she wouldn't have to worry about me. She asked me what my treatment plan was going to be but I didn't know at the time. I thought she was ok, but I could tell that she wasn't, so, I climbed onto the couch with her and I kissed her forehead and stroked her hair and just let her release the emotions that she had been holding inside. It was a blessed time with Ashley to be able to hold her only as a mother can and reassure her that everything would be ok.

I wasn't going to tell Sally until she had choir practice for Christmas Eve Mass because I didn't want to distract her from that. She and I were the only ones left at the dinner table and I was sitting across from her, praying and asking God if I should tell her. I felt that the opportunity was given to us for that reason. As I began telling her, she had a serious look on her face and didn't take her eyes off me, as I spoke. I know the Holy Spirit gave me the words that each of my girls needed to hear for them to accept God's will. Sally got up and came over to sit on my lap as she began to cry. I held her close and kissed her and told her that everything was going to be ok and that we just need to trust God's plan, because He knows what was best.

I struggled with myself, whether to tell Hailey before she began studying for her final exams or not. In the end, I figured, she would want to know. Again, I was given the words that she needed to hear and as I waited to hear her response, I recalled what she said when I told her about my spread of cancer to my bones. "It's like I'm immune to it," referring to the news about the cancer. I wondered what she was going to say this time, expecting something similar. She gave me her 'are you kidding me' look. She said she wasn't mad, because there wasn't anyone to be mad at, but she still was emotional. She came over to give me a hug, and she, too, asked what would happen next. I told her we needed to wait and see and pray. We talked until she felt a little better and felt that she had to get back to her homework.

So, then came the waiting game. Again.

I actually received a phone call from the doctor earlier than I had expected, which meant a lot to me since it was at the end of the workday on a Friday. The doctor asked how I was doing and I said I was good, and then asked him if I was going to be better after he shared what he found. He said, "Unfortunately, no."

I switched to "auto pilot" and quickly grabbed a pen and paper so I could write down what he said. Val was in the room with me and when the doctor said that he, indeed, found that the breast cancer cells had moved to the lining of my stomach;

I gave Val a 'thumbs down' sign. Val thought that meant the results came back negative. I wish.

So, another new journey begins. Again.

My oncologist thought it was best for me to continue with the same chemo shots that I had been receiving for my bone mets (cancer cells in my bones), to see if they would work on my stomach as well. The side effects from the shots were so minimal; I was all on board about trying to see if the drugs would work on the stomach, too. We tried that for a couple of months and then I had another stomach biopsy.

Although the reading of the biopsy would take some time, the doctor came into my room as I was waking up from anesthesia to tell me what she saw during the biopsy. I was looking forward to some good news from my latest stomach biopsy, even great news that the tumor had shrunk or even disappeared, but that wasn't the case. The doctor explained that she didn't see any improvement in the tumor, but also didn't see any new growth, which was a great blessing.

I was receiving the news pretty well, staying calm, but soon the tears came. I think my compromised status from being sedated contributed to the emotions. The drive home was quiet, and the only complete sentence I could put together in my head was, "Jesus, I trust in you." And I said that over and over and over again. Val held my hand all the way home and told me that everything was going to be okay. I believed him.

Dear Lord, as I get out of bed today, I know I'm stepping onto a battlefield. But I also know You've given me everything I need to stand firm. So in the power of Your Holy Spirit, I put on the armor of God: First, I place the helmet of salvation on my head. Protect my mind and imagination. Guard my eyes, allowing no sin to creep in. Focus my thoughts on the things of God. Let the breastplate of righteousness keep my heart and emotions safe. I pray that I won't be governed by my feelings, but by truth. Wrap Your Word around me like a belt. And safeguard me from error. I put on the sandals of peace to guide my steps. Plant my feet in Your truth. Empower me to stand firm against attack. Next, I take up the shield of faith. Protect me from Satan's fiery arrows. Place me shoulder to shoulder with Your army to oppose the Devil's schemes. Finally, I take up the sword of the Spirit, Your Word. Help me to read the Bible in a fresh, exciting way so I will always be ready to deflect attacks and pierce hearts with Your truth. (modified prayer from Ephesians 6:13-18)

I had several days throughout my journey that I needed to prepare myself for battle. But this bump in the road really tested me and I needed to guard myself against spiritual warfare! My Helmet protected me from thinking that the cancer had moved again and it would invade other parts of my body, especially my brain, which is a common place for breast cancer to spread to.

My heart was protected by the Breastplate of Righteousness so that it wouldn't be broken by the news of more cancer. My Belt of Truth in scripture continually reassured me of God's love and mercy for me. My Sandals gave me the peace in knowing that whatever God had planned for me, I would walk in my trust in Him, which was growing more and more each day. My Shield of Faith was large enough to ward off anything that would threaten my relationship with Jesus.

And finally, the Sword of the Spirit, God's word in my daily readings of the Gospel, strengthened me to fight off any attacks from the Devil. Much like the times before, the girls received the news with concern, a little more fear of losing me, but also, hope that the new chemo will help me.

Even though I received MANY, MANY prayers throughout those trying days, I didn't get the results I was hoping for. But, that was MY plan, not God's. My prayers HAD been answered.

Another PET scan showed that my bone mets had lowered. I had no new tumors. The hills and valleys that our family traveled through wasn't a vacation by any means, but it gave us more opportunities to spend time together, really beginning to understand that we are only promised today and to live today with love and joy in our hearts. Each time that we have been tested to see if we could continue to accept God's will, we have gained more traction in our faith and we continued to move forward with God by our side.

So that the proof of your faith, being more precious than gold which is perishable, even though tested by fire, may be found to result in praise and glory and honor at the revelation of Jesus Christ.

1 PETER 1:7

Rest Stop

I DIDN'T QUITE FEEL WELL ENOUGH to go to daily Mass one day, so I put on my comfy clothes and chose a movie to watch from Netflix. "A Greater Yes-the Amy Newhouse Story" caught my eye and as I read the description, I knew it might be an emotional movie, because it was about a 16 year old girl, who had a very bright future and was diagnosed with cancer. As I began watching the movie, I knew instantly, that God wanted me to stay home THAT day and watch THAT movie. The clincher was when Amy received good news that her tumor had shrunk and was able to leave the hospital after being there for 6 months. The date she left the hospital was April 14th. Tears quickly filled my eyes when I heard the date because it was the same date that I was watching the movie! What a God moment!

The similarities of Amy and I are quite incredible, yet her story is very different than mine, too. She wanted to make a difference by using her cancer journey and her faith to show her community that His plan is perfect and we need to have faith and hope in Him. She started a prayer group at her high school, which started with Amy, her boyfriend and one other student. As the movie goes on, the group continues to grow and the outpouring of prayer fills the halls at school. Amy befriends a loner, a boy who is really mad at the world, but he doesn't shake Amy's resolve. She continues to show her faith in him and eventually, this boy attends the prayer group. When he visits Amy in the hospital, where she has to spend time again, he asked her if she was tired of being hopeful. Amy's response was that hope was all she had left.

When Amy's cancer metastasized, she was lying in her hospital bed, wondering why God said "no" to a cure for her. She felt like she let everyone down by not being able to survive her cancer, and she shared that with her dad. What her dad told her made me almost gasp because it's the same goal that I want to achieve. "You've changed us all," he said.

Amy even asked why God had abandoned her. It was another God-incidence with it being Holy Week. Although I have never felt abandoned by God, it is the question that Jesus asked of his Father. At the end of the movie, Amy was narrating her final thoughts and how, even though she always was sure that God answered all of her prayers, she understood that "no" was an answer, too.

There may be a "no" for me someday, but I, too, trust that God will not answer my prayer in that way until He is satisfied with my work here and that I have earned a place in heaven with Him.

Welcome problems as perspective-lifters. My children tend to sleepwalk through their days until they bump into an obstacle that stymies them. If you encounter a problem with no immediate solution, your response to that situation will take you either up or down. You can lash out at the difficulty, resenting it and feeling sorry for yourself. This will take you down into a pit of self-pity. Alternatively, the problem can be a ladder, enabling you to climb up and see your life from My perspective. Viewed from above, the obstacle that frustrated you is only a light and momentary trouble. Once your perspective has been heightened, you can look away from the problem altogether. Turn toward Me, and see the Light of My Presence shining upon you. (Jesus Calling)

I read that reflection as the morning sun was shining on my face, and I could feel the warmth of His Presence. The house was quiet with everyone able to sleep in a bit. Even the dogs were sleeping. The ticking of the clock was almost the same tempo as my heartbeat as it provided a rhythm to my thoughts.

While I was drying off from my shower, I noticed there was more hair on the floor of the shower than usual. At first, I didn't give it much thought, but then I shushed my hands through my wet hair and more fell to the floor. I did it again and again, to see how much hair would fall out. It really wasn't a lot but it definitely was more than I usually lose in the shower. There was no panic or sad feeling; I think I even smiled as I realized that the next stage of treatment had arrived. With the very first chemo I had back in 2007, it was almost 100% chance that I would lose my hair and it was predicted that it would happen after my second treatment, which it did, on the dot. This time, though, it seemed that the hair loss may not be as prominent of a side effect. It may have been more of thinning hair. I had a lot of hair and I think I could go a long way before my hair would be noticeably thin. I did, however, make the decision that once it starts looking too thin, that I would shave it again. I had no problem doing that, at all.

I texted Val a picture of the amount of hair that had fallen out and said, "uh oh" and he immediately texted back, "I love you!" So, here we go again. Throughout the day, I would run my hand through my hair to see how much would be coming out, as if I was expecting the amount of hair to increase each time. When I would get up from the couch, I would look at the pillow to see how much hair was left there. After a while, I tried NOT to touch my hair because each time I did, there would be some on my hand and clothes. It was like I had just had my hair cut and those extra hairs that are left on my head that fall onto my eyelashes or on my Vaseline-covered lips and stick to them. It was a wee bit annoying.

I knew that I wanted Ashley to cut my hair if it was necessary and when I called her to ask if she was ready to do that for me, she agreed. I was actually looking forward to having her do it for me. I didn't know what would happen after that; if the shaving of the head would follow shortly or not. Again, there was no telling how much hair I may possibly lose and when. Ashley gave me an adorable pixie cut, trimming most of the colored hair off but there were still remnants of the color showing through the gray hair that was underneath. I called it my calico hair style, looking like a calico cat. Just like the first time that I had my hair cut short, waiting for it to fall out, I had pictures taken. This time though, it wasn't emotional for anyone.

I kept my eyes on the amount of hair leaving my head and it actually decreased! I thought it was odd, but didn't mind it at all! As it turned out, I didn't lose my hair and there was a point that there was more hair on my head than I had in almost 15 years! Not only was there a lot of hair, but it was really curly! I believe I had been blessed with chemo curl without losing my hair first. There is no scientific research to prove me right or wrong, but I just loved my curls!

Come away and rest a while.

MARK 6:31

Keep a Steady Pace

ONE DAY, I FOUND BLOOD IN MY STOOL. I wasn't quite sure what to think, but as you can imagine, many thoughts ran through my mind within seconds. I called Val to come home and take me to the Emergency Room. I thought that was my best chance of getting answers in a timely manner.

The ER doctor wanted me to have labs drawn and to have a CT scan. As I was getting lined up for the scan, the tech came out of his protective room to move my miraculous medal, which I very rarely take off my neck. It seemed that, although Mary was protecting me, she was within the scanning area. We exchanged words about Mary wanting to be part of the excitement and the tech carefully moved Mary to the side of my neck. The scan took just several minutes and I was back in my room, alone. I watched a little TV to pass the time. Val ran to his office and had planned on being back shortly. When the doctor came in and sat down, and began telling me what the radiologist saw on my scan. I understood what he was telling me until he started using words like, "indicates that the cancer may have moved." I squinted at him as if that would help understand what he was saying. It didn't. Thankfully, Val walked in and I asked the doctor to repeat what he just told me, which he did. When I looked at Val, his eyes were red and he stood up and took my hand into his. I looked back at him, smiling a "here we go again" smile through my tears. The plan was to talk with a gastroenterologist and see what he thought should be done. I began a full fledge cry. I tried to keep it together until he left, but couldn't. Val climbed onto the hospital bed and held me. It was a familiar, too familiar, feeling that makes my mind race into many directions. It was 3:10 and I really wanted to pray the Divine Mercy Chaplet, so with his green, 'Grandma Stanton' rosary, Val led us through the Chaplet. So often, when I listen to the chaplet, I hear such heart wrenching stories of suffering and I am always very thankful that I am not one of them. But, at that moment, I felt almost as desperate as those who call into Relevant Radio as I answered Val's prompts of, "For the sake of His sorrowful passion" with, "Have mercy on us and on the whole world." I ended with the five words that bring me peace, "Jesus, I trust in You." When we finished the chaplet, I felt better and I thanked God for making me aware of the time and how I could ask for His mercy when I needed it the most.

Two doctors came in to talk with me. First, a gastro surgeon, asked me to tell him the story I had told several times already. He was very pleased with what I told him and was confident that my situation wasn't as serious as previously thought. We liked to hear that! He left and another doctor came in several minutes later. He opened up the closet door and pulled out a folding chair and sat down next to my bed. He began by recapping what he and the gastro doctor had just discussed, laying out my options and being very personable about it. The more he said, the better Val and I felt. He even said that the possibility that the cancer had moved may have been over cautiously diagnosed.

After having a couple more tests done, we waited for more results. I spent my days waiting, being a mom, laughing with the girls, making meals, getting things done, but if I stopped for a moment, my mind traveled to the dark side and I let Satan enter my thoughts and soon, I would be holding back tears of the unknown. I went to confession and I knew, going in, that I was going to break down, which I did. I think I just needed to be able to speak the words that were burning in my heart to someone, other than my family. I told the priest that I KNEW that God would take care of me. I repeated that several times, but what was bothering me was that there were times when I just couldn't pray.

The priest took his Bible and looked up Romans 8:26 and read, "*In the same way, the Spirit too comes to the aid of our weakness; for we do not know how to pray as we ought, but the Spirit itself intercedes with inexpressible groanings. And the one who searches hearts knows what is the intention of the Spirit, because it intercedes for the holy ones according to God's will.*"

He then, went on to tell me something that made me feel much better, even though it made me cry more. He said that I am so close to Jesus at those moments and He knows that I love Him, even if I can't tell Him that at the time. I remember reading that when we suffer, we are experiencing the suffering that Jesus did for us and that brings us closer to Him. At those moments when I feel I really cannot pray, I still am, just by saying, "Jesus, I trust in You." And when I cannot even mouth the words, He knows my heart. What comfort it is to know that my relationship with Jesus is so grounded that without saying a word, He knows the trust I have in Him.

I truly don't think I suffer often, but as Father spoke those words, I surrendered to the fact that I do suffer, more spiritually than physically at times. I don't like the thought of that because I feel that my spiritual life has grown so deep and strong and that I should be able to handle whatever comes my way. What I don't remember is that Satan LOVES to sneak into my thoughts but gets very mad when my love for God is shining light on others, so he has to work really hard to penetrate my relationship with God. I can trust that God will help me drive Satan out of my thoughts even in my weakest hour.

> *Therefore, since we are surrounded by so great a cloud of witnesses, let us also lay aside every weight and the sin that clings so closely, and let us run with perseverance the race that is set before us, looking to Jesus the pioneer and perfecter of our faith, who for the sake of the joy that was set before him endured the cross, disregarding its shame, and has taken his seat at the right hand of the throne of God. Consider him who endured such hostility against himself from sinners, so that you may not grow weary or lose heart. In your struggle against sin you have not yet resisted to the point of shedding your blood. (Hebrews 12:1-4)*

We rejoice in our sufferings, knowing that suffering produces endurance, and endurance produces character and character produces hope.

ROMANS 5: 3-4

Retreat! Retreat!

A T THE ANNUAL MOM'S RETREAT at my parish, we began the evening in the main sanctuary. Father Jim graciously joined us for Adoration. He processed in, holding the Monstrance with his covered hands, in respect for the holiness of Jesus' Presence before him. He placed Jesus on the altar and proceeded to read us the story of the woman who had been inflicted by continuous hemorrhaging for twelve years.

> Now there was a woman who had been suffering from hemorrhages for twelve years. She had endured much under many physicians, and had spent all that she had; and she was no better, but rather grew worse. She had heard about Jesus, and came up behind him in the crowd and touched his cloak, for she said, "If I but touch his clothes, I will be made well." Immediately her hemorrhage stopped; and she felt in her body that she was

healed of her disease. Immediately aware that power had gone forth from him, Jesus turned about in the crowd and said, "Who touched my clothes?" And his disciples said to him, "You see the crowd pressing in on you; how can you say, 'Who touched me?'" He looked all around to see who had done it. But the woman, knowing what had happened to her, came in fear and trembling, fell down before him, and told him the whole truth. He said to her, "Daughter, your faith has made you well; go in peace, and be healed of your disease." (Mark 5:25-34)

I was sitting in the pews, directly in front of Jesus and for a while I couldn't take my eyes off of Jesus. Then, tears began to fill my eyes as I was basking in His love and mercy. For several minutes I continued to allow my tears to slowly travel down my cheek as I smiled.

Before my first retreat, I didn't know much about Adoration. Now, I look forward to my hour each week, when I can sit with our Lord and adore Him and bring my prayers to Him. I didn't attend weekday Masses. Now, I attend at least two daily Masses during the week and I can follow the stories in the Bible much easier, along with awesome homilies from Fr. Tom. Before the retreat, I didn't pray the rosary at all. Now, Val and I pray a rosary every morning together. Before the retreat, I didn't go to confession on a regular basis. I actually only went a couple of times a year. Now, I receive the sacrament of reconciliation once a month, which makes my life more peaceful. I didn't go from zero to 60 in ten seconds flat. It took some time. My consecration to Mary encouraged me to go to first Saturday Mass and reconciliation as part of my commitment to my consecration to her.

There was a lot of spiritual growth in six years. I went from not wanting to say anything about my faith at my first retreat, to being a table leader, to being the facilitator for the retreat!

In 2015, my role was a table leader again and as a leader, we were asked to model what to do during Adoration on Friday night in case there were women there for the first time, just like I was 6 years prior. Again, the story about the faithful woman wanting to just touch the hem of Jesus' clothes was read. It is a powerful story for the mothers to hear because, we know, we all have areas in our lives that could use some healing. I was the first to walk up to the monstrance and kneel before Jesus. The altar table had been dressed with the beautiful gold monstrance and a simple white cloth that gently wrapped the stand of the monstrance. The white cloth represented Jesus' tunic. I knelt close to the altar so that I could touch the cloth. I held it in my hand as I looked up at Jesus. Time stood still. As my eyes were fixed on Jesus, I heard the words in my heart, "Rhonda, let me heal you." I placed my face into the white cloth and began to cry softly.

Up until this point on my cancer journey, believe it or not, I did not pray to be healed from cancer. Call me crazy, but I thought my mission in life was to serve God by serving others on their journey with a cross, specifically cancer, by being an example of how joyful life can be, living with stage 4 cancer. Don't get me wrong, I prayed for good test results. I prayed for pain to go away. I prayed that tumor markers would go down. But, ultimately, I prayed for acceptance of God's will.

That night in the sanctuary, kneeling before Christ, I accepted His offer. I did not know exactly what that meant but my heart had opened to being healed. I began praying the following prayer:

Prayer to Our Lady

*Dear Blessed Mother, teach me your loving acceptance of the
    divine will.*
*May I be a true servant to the Lord, generous in doing all that
    pleases Him.*
*Graciously, intercede for me before His throne. Obtain for me,
    if it be His holy will,*
The favors and blessings I recommend to your motherly heart.
(my special intentions)

I ask that I accept whatever Jesus has planned for me and And
if it is your son's will for me to be completely healed, I will give
Him more honor, more glory, and more praise.

Hail Mary, full of grace, the Lord is with thee.
*Blessed art thou, among women and blessed is the fruit of thy
    womb, Jesus.*
*Holy Mary, Mother of God, pray for us sinners, now and at the
    hour of our death.*
Amen.
Virgin Gentle in Mercy, pray for us.
(Franciscan Mission Associates)

Daughter, your faith has healed you.

MARK 5:34

Work in Progress

When it was evening on that day, the first day of the week, and the doors of the house where the disciples had met were locked for fear of the Jews, Jesus came and stood among them and said, "Peace be with you." After he said this, he showed them his hands and his side. Then the disciples rejoiced when they saw the Lord. Jesus said to them again, "Peace be with you. As the Father has sent me, so I send you." When he had said this, he breathed on them and said to them, "Receive the Holy Spirit. If you forgive the sins of any, they are forgiven them; if you retain the sins of any, they are retained."

But Thomas (who was called the Twin), one of the twelve, was not with them when Jesus came. So the other disciples told him, "We have seen the Lord." But he said to them, "Unless I see the mark of the nails in his hands, and put my finger in the mark of the nails and my hand in his side, I will not believe."

A week later his disciples were again in the house, and Thomas was with them. Although the doors were shut, Jesus came and stood among them and said, "Peace be with you." Then he said to Thomas, "Put your finger here and see my hands. Reach

out your hand and put it in my side. Do not doubt but believe."
Thomas answered him, "My Lord and my God!" Jesus said to him,
"Have you believed because you have seen me? Blessed are those
who have not seen and yet have come to believe." (John 20:19-29)

THOMAS –FOREVER KNOWN as 'Doubting Thomas'—may have been labeled a little unjustly, but I can understand how it could have happened. He wasn't there when Jesus appeared to the apostles, which made it difficult for him to believe what he heard, even though he had been with Jesus and the other apostles for three years.

Regardless of what Thomas was known for or for the fact that he doubted that Jesus had risen from the grave, he was the first one who identified Jesus as, "My Lord and my God." But I'm sure Thomas was not the only one who proclaimed these four words. Whether it was the healing of the man at the beautiful gate, the hemorrhaging woman, or the parable of the prodigal son, Jesus is teaching us that God's mercy and love is never ending. After the oncologist that I had been seeing for the last 8 years retired, my new doctor scheduled a PET scan to have a starting point with our new relationship. I was excited to see if my prayers were being heard. As you remember, I had an experience at a retreat at my parish that made me want to pray to be healed. Still accepting whatever God had planned for me, but willing to accept His healing, too. I had also been listening to Relevant Radio, especially at 3:00 each day to listen to Drew Mariani as he prayed the Divine Mercy Chaplet. So many times over the past several years, I have heard about miracles happening when people prayed the Chaplet. I believed that could happen to me, too, so when it was time to hear of the results of my PET scan, I was ready to hear whatever the results would be. I have always gone into those appointments with the open mind of hearing news of my cancer being more serious. Not expecting it, but preparing for the possibility of it. I usually don't bring Val along, either, but that time, I wanted him to meet my new doctor.

So, when the doctor came in and began by saying that the results were good and went down the list of results; all were a blur to me because I never focus on those results. She then came to the "Impression" section of the report:

1. *"Stable, no new skeletal lesions." My bones have remained stable for many months and it was a blessing to hear that they remained that way.*

2. *"No soft tissue abnormalities. Overall there is no evidence of active disease."*

Wait, what?

"Soft tissue means my stomach, right?" I asked, looking at Val with almost a confused look on my face. Did I hear her correctly?

NO EVIDENCE OF ACTIVE DISEASE ANYWHERE IN MY BODY! ANYWHERE!

As wonderful, absolutely wonderful as the news was, I had a hard time believing what I just heard. Just exactly like Thomas! MY LIFE WAS SUPPOSED TO BE…That thought made me feel bad, almost like I was lying to Mary when I prayed. Even though Thomas had been with Jesus for three years, learning from Him, praying with Him, and serving Him, it was still difficult to believe such news of Jesus appearing to the apostles. There I was, learning from Jesus for years, praying to Him, and serving Him, and now, my prayers were answered and I was questioning Jesus' power to heal me! I knew that wasn't true! I KNEW how much He loved me, and He showed that by dying on the cross for me and for you!

So, where did I go from there? I had been the face of 'living with stage 4 cancer with joy' for the last few years and now what was I? I imagined living with cancer for the rest of my life and I had pretty much accepted the fact that I would probably die of cancer, too. The news was blowing my mind! God was making it very clear that HE was in charge of my life, not me! I bet He was chuckling as He compared me to His friend Thomas!

My special intention for my Prayer to Our Lady became, "Please show me *how* to honor your Son!" I thanked Jesus and His Mother, over and over again, through tears of joy, while shaking my head at times, and I looked forward to see which direction they would be leading me!

My treatment remained the same because it had been working wonderfully for me. I had to admit, when the decision was made to continue with the same schedule and chemo, I was a little something—not sure if disappointed would be the right word—but I had thoughts of not having to need any more chemotherapy. Don't get me wrong, I was very pleased with the results and I was very happy to continue with my chemo. My quality of life had been outstanding and the side effects had also been very minimal.

The story about doubting Thomas is a story that every one of us can relate to. Every one of us has thought, "I can't believe it." But, just as Jesus confirmed Thomas' faith, He can do the same for us. Jesus wants us to be like Thomas, trying to overcome our human nature to doubt, but He also wants us to be like Thomas and say, "Jesus, you are my Lord and my God."

May the God of hope fill you with
all joy and peace in believing.

ROMANS 15:13

This Is the Way

JUST TWO WEEKS TO THE DAY of receiving the amazing news that my prayers were answered and I no longer had any active cancer in my body, my mom called me from Florida to tell me that she had ovarian cancer. My new prayers of "now what would you like me to do for you?" were answered quite quickly but I would have never thought they would be answered that way. I had just finished having chemo and was at Goodwill, getting my weekly enjoyment of looking for treasures when I saw that I had missed her phone call and saw the text, "call me, please…HUGS". I called her without even thinking that she may have the results from the procedure she had done earlier in the week to have fluid in her abdomen being drained. She answered and I automatically asked how she was, her reply was "fine", then she went right into what she needed to tell me. I'm walking around the store, looking for aisles that didn't have anyone in them because I didn't want to be rude talking on the phone especially about such a personal subject. I thought about going out to my car, but I had items that I wanted to purchase in my shopping cart and didn't know what to do with them. It was fine.

We spoke for less than 10 minutes but our conversation was calm and faith-filled. I felt she knew she could count on me to understand exactly what she was feeling, and I did. It became very clear to me that I was healed in order to show everyone that God is merciful and generous. I was healed to show others how powerful prayer and faithfulness is. And, I was healed to pave the way of hope and healing for my mom and my family, as she began her journey with cancer.

Mom's plan was to see her doctor in Florida, where they live half of the year and where she had her tests done, and then head home as soon as possible, which was a couple weeks earlier than they had planned. In my head, I was already planning on flying down to be with her, to help in any way she needed, but I was letting her make that decision.

I remembered a week earlier, talking with mom about her procedure to remove the fluid in her abdomen and I didn't like being so far away from her. I recognized, once again, that I would rather be the one to suffer than to 'watch' or hear about my mom hurting. When someone we love suffers, it also causes suffering in us; an emotional suffering, sometimes gut wrenching suffering. The world sometimes forgets about the caretakers, the significant others, the family members, whoever takes care of anyone who is going through a difficult time. Within 30 minutes of saying goodbye to mom on the phone, she texted me to say that she and dad were packing up and coming home immediately. I was relieved to know she was on her way home.

The rest of my day was spent thinking about mom and what was probably going through her head. I thought a lot about my dad and my siblings, too. Mom called each one, along with her sisters. I remember dreading those phone calls. I still do. I called mom later in the day to see how she was doing. She was quite amazing. She rattled off what she had been doing all day: washing clothes, bed linens, and towels; saying goodbye to her neighbors; giving away the food in her refrigerator that would spoil, calling and cancelling appointments and tee times. Amazing, but, that is what we have to do, life goes on! Her pace was probably just a little faster than most ;)

Mom and dad arrived home a few days later, and it was so good to hold my mom tight and let her know that everything was going to be ok. There were appointments set up for her and I asked mom and dad if they would like me to go with them since I knew some of what they would probably hear from her doctors. I was so glad to be able to take one of mom's hands into mine and walk the path of cancer with her, while Jesus took her other hand.

Mom had exploratory surgery and what they found wasn't very good. Her entire abdominal cavity was covered with a thin coat of cancer cells that originated from her ovaries. There was no way to remove anything surgically so chemotherapy was first on the agenda to shrink and/or kill the cancer cells within her. So, to prepare her for her difficult journey, I bought her a beautiful miraculous medal for her to wear so she would feel our Blessed Mother's presence and intercession when mom needed her.

The entire summer was filled with trips to the doctor, stays in the hospital, and most of her days, sleeping in the bed we made in the living room of their house. Their bedroom was on the second floor and it was too much for mom to go up and down the stairs so we placed a mattress on top of the pull-out couch, which actually worked really well. It was really tough to see my mom as weak as she was. I know there were moments when our family was very worried about her, especially my dad. He would sit in his chair and watch mom breath, just to make sure she was. Dad was absolutely amazing throughout mom's treatment. For fifty nine years, Mom pretty much had done all of the grocery shopping, making of the meals, and doing the other daily duties, but she wasn't able to do any of that during her treatment. Dad didn't skip a beat when he needed to do those things.

There were many dark days for mom, and I'm sure for dad, as well. I even went into the darkness at times, when mom would have a set back. Darkness can be so lonely and scary. But, when I could turn toward God and the light he provides, I could see that our final destination is heaven and if that meant that mom was going to meet our heavenly Father sooner than we would want her to, it wasn't as scary.

> *I am the light of the world, whoever*
> *follows me will not walk in darkness.*
>
> John 8:12

Need a Tow Truck?

V AL AND I HAD PLANNED a simple overnight in a Bed
and Breakfast in a small town a couple of hours away
from home, to celebrate our 23rd wedding anniversary
in June. We looked forward to some quiet time with each other
in the gorgeous mansion and then enjoying the five course
breakfast that we heard raves about the next morning before we
headed to the Shrine of Our Lady of Guadalupe in La Crosse,
Wisconsin. On our way down, we stopped for lunch and as
we continued on our short trek, I began feeling like the lunch
I ate did not agree with me. I brushed it off as the feeling I get
periodically with my digestive system. Do you remember GG?
By the time we got to the B & B, I was feeling pretty lousy and
couldn't wait to get up to our room and lie down. Of course, the
proprietor wanted to show us the house and all of its amenities

before he showed us our room. I was thankful that I made it to the room, the bathroom in particular, in time. I just wasn't feeling better like I usually do after eating something that disagreed with me. We didn't go out for dinner, in fact, Val went out to grab something that sounded good to me, which was really nothing and after about four hours of wondering what to do, I finally told Val that I needed to go to the Emergency Room at the local hospital. That decision scared me. I remembered passing the hospital on the way into town so I knew it was only a short distance away and I was very thankful for that. Val asked me if I wanted him to drive me to our hometown hospital and I told him I would never be able to handle the pain for the two hour drive home!

I was checked into the ER as the pain continued to get worse. I hadn't been in that kind of pain before, which scared me. Vitals were taken, questions were asked and all I wanted was some relief from the pain. I remember saying to Val, "I offer up this pain for…" and I rattled off as many names as I could. I might as well make my pain worth something! I think that was the first time I had thought of offering up my suffering for someone else while I was actually in pain. I was surprised that I thought of it because it was very difficult to think clearly.

The doctor thought it could be kidney stones or my appendix. I had never experienced kidney stones but I heard they could be very painful and I had never an issue with my appendix so it, too, sounded like a possibility. I was given some pain medication and I found relief and was very thankful for that. Labs were drawn, I had a CT scan and it was decided that I needed to be admitted. By this time, it was after midnight and I sent Val back to the B & B for a few hours of sleep. Fortunately, I was able to sleep for a few hours, too.

After hours of trying to connect my doctor in Winona to

doctors at my hospital to compare CT scans, it was decided that I needed an appendectomy, and by that time, ASAP! It turned out that my appendix had a slight rupture, possibly due to the delay in surgery. We will never know that and it doesn't matter anymore. I spent three days in the hospital in Winona. Val stayed with me for a little while after my surgery but then needed to go home to be with Sally. (By the way, he never got to enjoy the five course breakfast the next morning because he came back to the hospital very early.) I have to say that even though I wasn't up for visitors, it still seemed a little lonely being so far away from home. My care was outstanding and the doctor checked in on me several times. He was very thorough and was concerned about my compromised immune system, due to the cancer.

I was released into the care of Sally and Val and the drive home from Winona wasn't as bad as I thought it might be. It was good to be home and I looked forward to celebrating Sally's 14th birthday and our anniversary the next day. Unfortunately, my stay at home didn't last very long, just a little more than 24 hours. I was experiencing the "signs to watch out for" and ended up going to the ER again, this time was at St. Francis, my hospital. After examining me and answering the multitude of questions, I was again, admitted to the hospital with the possibility of an infection from my surgery, something that my doctor from Winona warned be about.

Four more days in the hospital, hooked up to antibiotics, more scans and ultrasounds, a clear liquid diet in case I needed more surgery, still healing from my surgery and dealing with the symptoms of infection, I wasn't a happy camper. I had missed out on our stay in the B & B, missed celebrating Sally's birthday and our anniversary, and I missed Father's Day, which was the following day. Just as in Winona, I wasn't feeling the greatest for seeing visitors, but I so longed for interaction with my family. My mom and dad visited and so did Val, Ashley and Sally. My sister, Renee, also came when I was finally feeling well enough to visit. Even when they were there, I still felt alone, knowing that they would be able to go home and I wasn't.

> *Then Peter came and said to Him, "Lord, how often shall my brother sin against me and I forgive him? Up to seven times?" Jesus said to him, "I do not say to you, up to seven times, but up to seventy times seven. "My heavenly Father will also do the same to you, if each of you does not forgive his brother from your heart." (Matthew 18:21-22, 35)*

Jesus may have sounded quite harsh in this parable but He was trying to show how important it is to forgive those who have sinned against you. Seven times or seven times seventy times, it's the same thing: every time. We have all been hurt at some time in our lives, and sometimes that hurt can stay with us for a long, long time. If we don't deal with our pain, it can become a recurring nightmare. If we do not deal with the hurt by forgiving those who have hurt us, it's as if we are spinning our wheels, trying to move forward in life but we are getting nowhere.

We don't have to live like we're stuck in the mud! Forgiveness is the traction we need. And if the hurt causes us to get stuck again, forgive again. And again. Seven times seventy times, if necessary. I believe I have a great relationship with my siblings, five sisters and two brothers. We all live within 30 minutes of each other and we see each other on holidays and other celebrations. We were all raised by both of our parents but our mom was the one who took us to our Catholic Church every Sunday. My dad was raised Lutheran but rarely went to his church. All eight of us kids are at various levels of our belief in God and heaven and I'm pretty sure they are all clear as to how incredibly important my faith is to me. So, it surprised my when I found myself angry with some of them when I didn't hear from then during a stay I had in the hospital.

This is where the connection of the parable to my experience comes in. I said that I didn't want visitors but I was very sad that I didn't hear from some of my siblings. No phone call, no email, no text. I'm not sure if they were too busy, forgot, didn't think I wanted to be 'bothered', didn't know what to say, or what. But I was hurt. That hurt remained in my heart for weeks and I finally needed to do something about it. I went to confession. I needed to forgive them so I could let go of that hurt and have a clean heart. I didn't like being mad at them and they had no idea that they had hurt me. I cried through my confession, feeling so guilty of my feelings because I love them so much and I felt that I was hurting them by being mad at them. My experience in the hospital had taken a toll on my mental health, as well as my physical health and I think that made my feelings even more difficult to put into words. Of course, Father, on behalf of Jesus, had kind words to say to me and helped me release the sadness, guilt, and hurt from my heart. I left the confessional feeling much lighter and peaceful.

I had a choice to make. I could have been like the king in the parable, and forgive my siblings with grace and mercy, or I could have been like the servant and make my siblings "pay" for not communicating with me. My faith allowed me to see that what I was feeling and experiencing was not my usual way of looking at life, so I chose the path of love and mercy over one covered in bitterness. Sometimes, all we need is to take just one small step to forgive a hurt. Other times, we need to take a number of steps, over a long period of time, before we get our heart to a place where we can forgive. Whatever it takes, as long as we are trying to move forward, our heavenly Father will help us along.

You may feel hurt by the cross you have been given. You hurt because it wasn't the plan you had in your life. You may be very angry at God for the cross he has placed upon you, and that pain may be too great to forgive God right now. But God can see into your heart, He knows how you feel and He still loves you very deeply. When you can accept God's perfect plan for you, your hurt will lessen and you will be able to continue on the path that God has chosen for you with peace in your heart.

So whatever your situation is, imagine our heavenly Father throwing a tow rope to you, to help pull you out of that place where you can't seem to budge from. Grab onto the rope, tell Him how hard it is to hold on, and ask Him for help. Give Him time to pull you out, just as He has given you time to ask for help.

> *Be careful how you think; your life*
> *is shaped by your thoughts.*
> PROVERBS 4:23

Handicapped Parking

WHEN I WAS RELEASED FROM ST. FRANCIS, I was told that I could not receive any chemotherapy until I had a colonoscopy to make sure that there were no other issues with my colon. I had colonoscopies before and I knew the prep wasn't the greatest but I realized that it must be important enough to have another one. I scheduled my procedure with the same doctor that had seen me in the hospital and he was also the doctor who removed my gallbladder in 2012. I felt very comfortable with him. It was difficult to schedule a time since I had to take into account the days of prep leading up to the procedure. There were activities every weekend so I had to choose which event that I was going to have to sacrifice not eating the yummy food in order to follow the prep guidelines.

He took biopsy samples in order to be sure that everything was as good as it looked. I remember the doctor telling me, as

I was waking up, that he would call me with the results of the biopsy. I had forgotten that he said that, until he called me on a Friday afternoon as I was at my mom's house, picking up some golf clubs for the girls to use the next day at a golf tourney/ family reunion. He asked me how I was and I replied, "You tell me!" He replied by telling me that the biopsy showed that the breast cancer cells had moved to my colon. I didn't say a word. It seemed like minutes ticked by, but it was for just a second or two before I could manage to speak. I was very thankful, as most times in the past, that I was given the grace to be clear headed and ask appropriate questions and keep calm on the phone. The doctor suggested I make an appointment to see my oncologist and I told him that I had one already set up for the following week, in anticipation of hearing good news and to be able to begin chemo again. Well, I guess the second part of that was true, I WOULD be starting chemo again, probably a new one, though.

I thanked the doctor and ended our phone call and I sat in my car for a few minutes, my mind racing with many thoughts. Thoughts that I have had before, each time I received a phone call with news that my cancer had spread. Should I call Val? No, he was in the middle of a meeting. When would I see the girls to tell them? Oh no, the golf tourney would have so many people there, should I tell them? I didn't want to put a damper on the fun day. What kind of chemo would I need? Would I get sick from it? Lose my hair? And on and on, the thoughts went.

I went into the house, where my mom had been resting and I sat on the side of her bed and told her about my news. She patted the pillow next to her and motioned for me to lie down next to her. My mom, who was still recovering from her cancer surgery and needing a lot of care, was being the mama I needed her to be at that moment, caring for her child who was hurting. I snuggled up to her and she put her arm around me and I just cried. She had a new perspective of my journey since she was her own cancer journey, receiving phone calls with disappointing news. It gave me such comfort knowing that she could understand how I was feeling, better than she could in the past.

Once I gathered myself again, I was about to get into my car and head home and my dad came home and met me by my car. I told him my news, and he, too, had a new appreciation for my situation. He held me tight and told me he loved me and that everything would be ok. I cried some more but I believed him. I left him with a smile on my face, but there wasn't a smile in my heart. The drive home was filled with more thoughts and more tears.

I have been blessed with peace and acceptance with my cancer journey, even though I have had moments of sadness and fear. But, the latest finding of more cancer really took me to a place where I didn't like to be. I wasn't sure why, either. The past month had been difficult for me, with my appendix surgery, the extended time in the hospital and how long it had taken for me to feel good again. I never once thought that God had abandoned me or was punishing me or anything like that. I just couldn't get a handle on my emotions and I still needed to share my news! Val and I sat on our patio as I told him of the latest discovery. We sat there for quite a while. Some of the time I would try to put into words what was going on in my head, some of the time, Val would reassure me that everything was going to ok, and some of the time, we just sat in silence, with tears running down my cheeks.

I could just tell you to go back to the chapters where I had to tell the girls and re-read those paragraphs about how difficult it was, but I think you get the picture by now. Timing was everything and we didn't have much of it. I was able to tell Sally, since she still lived at home, but Ashley and Hailey did not, and I was not going to tell them over the phone. Thankfully, Hailey came home that night and I asked Val if he would tell her. She had a tough day at work, was tired, had homework to do and all I could think of was that I was going to add to her bad day. I didn't see Ashley until we met up at the golf tourney the next day. With 100 family members surrounding us, all waiting for a group picture, I leaned over to her and whispered the news in her ear. Tears began to fall and others were noticing and I felt really bad that she was hurting. I just needed to tell her before she heard it from someone else. With that, the news began to spread, which was almost better so that I didn't have to tell as many people. It may sound silly, how much I have shared with you about the difficulty I have had telling others, but I don't think there is anyone who enjoys sharing bad news and I have had to share bad news so many times.

> *He entered again into a synagogue; and a man was there whose hand was withered. They were watching Him to see if He would heal him on the Sabbath, so that they might accuse Him. He said to the man with the withered hand, "Get up and come forward!" And He said to them, "Is it lawful to do good or to do harm on the Sabbath, to save a life or to kill?" But they kept silent. After looking around at them with anger, grieved at their hardness of heart, He said to the man, "Stretch out your hand." And he stretched it out, and his hand was restored. The Pharisees went out and immediately began conspiring with the Herodians against Him, as to how they might destroy Him. (Mark 3:1-10)*

Have you ever experienced something that could be considered a "withered hand" in your life? It could be an accident that has left you partially paralyzed, needing a wheelchair or walker to help you with your physical needs. Maybe it was an emotional issue that hindered you from living a joyful life. Maybe it was a time when your faith was "withered" and left you far from the Lord. If you're reading this book, I imagine your answer would be yes to any of the possibilities. Living with a "withered hand" like the man in Mark's gospel, may make each day seem like you're living a handicapped life.

Imagine if you met someone, like Jesus, who could heal you from the pain and suffering, whether it was physical, emotional or spiritual? Wouldn't you take a chance for healing? That man did! When Jesus called out to him as He stretched out his hand to the man, he didn't hesitate and his life was full and rich again. He didn't need to beg in the streets any longer. There was no more disability to keep him from following Jesus.

Jesus wants us to stretch out our hand toward His and take hold of it. He wants to heal us. He doesn't want us to be living a life that isn't in His plan, but one with love and mercy, and forgiveness. I grabbed hold of Jesus' hand long ago, and I am not letting go! And neither is He!

Call on me in times of trouble and I will
rescue you and you will honor me.

PSALM 50:15

Final Destination

"In my Father's house there are many dwelling places. If it were not so, would I have told you that I go to prepare a place for you? And if I go and prepare a place for you, I will come again and will take you to myself, so that where I am, there you may be also. And you know the way to the place where I am going." (John 14:2-4)

WE CAN EXPERIENCE BITS AND PIECES of heaven each time we stop to pray and give thanks for all that God has given us. Doing anything that pleases Him deepens our relationship with Him. The moments that we can experience what heaven might be like also helps us when we are having difficult times in our lives. It's important to picture in our minds, heaven and all its glory, especially when we need to find the joy in our lives. Some think that heaven is full of angels, laying around, playing harps and singing. It's a beautiful image and I'm sure that there are artists that have painted pictures of that description! But, if we read scripture, we know that heaven is a busy place with God always working and right by his side, are his children.

As I am writing this, my treatment for the metastatic breast cancer that has moved to my bones (but it is currently inactive, praise God), my stomach lining and cecum (that remain thickened), and my colon (which gives me the most discomfort) is two oral pills that I take daily that are doing a pretty good job at keeping the tumor markers down. However, at each monthly visit with my oncologist, we discuss my options and whether or not to change chemotherapy drugs. There are currently a few more options for me and I am confident that there will continue to be more options as researchers find more drugs that will work in my situation.

Over the past several years, especially since my recurrence, I have had many opportunities to witness to others, my faith and trust in the Lord. A couple of years after my original diagnosis, I felt called to start up a ministry at my church, with a fellow breast cancer survivor, to pray for women who were diagnosed with breast cancer. It soon evolved into a general cancer ministry, praying for not only women, but men and children, too. *The Pink Prayer Warriors* will journey alongside those who are embarking into new territory. Having been down "that road before", I was able to understand some of their fears and anxieties, but most of all, I was there for them in prayer. Our ministry grew and so did the warriors that we prayed for. We currently have over 350 warriors. Being part of this community, it is unfortunate, but expected to lose some of our warriors to cancer. Being with them at the end of their earthly journey has been a privilege for me and has helped me see the beauty of passing from this life to the next. And as we celebrated their lives, I began planning how I wanted my life to be celebrated. I have chosen songs that I enjoy singing and readings that have meant something to me, and who I would like to sing and read. I have no idea when Jesus will call me home, but none of us have that knowledge. But, I think it's a good idea to have plans of what we would like read, sung or displayed, to celebrate our lives because it will make things easier for our loved ones during a difficult time.

My perspective on life continues to evolve and there are days that I am truly living in the moment, not knowing what the next moment will bring. I am grateful for the many awesome days, the good days, and I accept the days when I have to stay close to home because I don't feel well.

But the joy in my life continues to increase each day with the blessings that have been placed along my journey. I am blessed that I can recognize them and I'm doubly blessed that I have my family and friends to share them with. I don't give much thought to the seriousness of my health and the possibility of God calling me home sooner than I have planned, but knowing what is waiting for me in heaven gives me such peace that the end doesn't scare me like it did in the past. That peace has come from having an intimate relationship with Jesus and His mother Mary. I want you to have a relationship with Jesus and His mother, too. I want you to have peace in knowing that His plan is perfect, even though you cannot see it or understand it. Trust Him. He knows what is best for you. All of the tough days, the heavy burdens, the difficult moments, are preparing you for the most beautiful eternal life that is just around the bend…

Set your minds on things above, not on earthly things.

Colossians 3:2

Strong Foundation

AT MY MONTHLY VISIT to my oncologist, we had a heart-to-heart talk about my future. The last couple of months had been a bit tougher for me and my thoughts were drawn to my passing more than before. My doctor explained to me that the cancer that was probably in my entire digestive system was very serious because at any time, the cancer cells could cause a rupture in the intestines and it could be very difficult to find and repair it. She also said that if that happened, my health could spiral down very quickly. I took a deep breath. I was not expecting to hear anything like that but that is why I was asking the questions of what to expect so I would have some idea of what could possibly happen to me.

My next question was when she thought it would be time to talk with my girls about this and she said the time was then. Another deep breath was needed which was followed by a few tears and a tissue. That didn't mean that my dying was particularly close, but there was no reason to wait to talk with the girls. Throughout my entire journey, I had been as open and honest as I could be with them and at that point, it was very important to be transparent with what would possibly happen.

I had changed chemotherapy options a many times, each drug being effective for about six months. At that point, I was taking six oral pills daily with possibly adding another pill to get to the maximum strength of that drug. The side effects were getting more prominent. I had the beginning signs of neuropathy, which is a strange sensitivity and tingling in my fingertips and feet. It wasn't a common side effect from that particular drug but everybody reacts differently.

When I shared my new information with Val, we were sitting in our den, which was filled with prayer. Everywhere you looked, our faith was hanging on the wall, sitting on a shelf or gently lighting the room. I was able to convey most of the conversation I had with my doctor with Val, until I saw tears in his eyes. That brought me to tears. I tried to continue talking but needed to be closer to him, so I climbed onto his chair with him and he held me in his arms and we quietly let the tears fall freely.

I couldn't keep this from the girls. I wanted to gather them and tell them. I wanted to tell them all together so they would all hear the same words. I wanted my son- in-law, Danny to be there and Alex, Hailey's boyfriend to be there because it would be them that the girls would go to for support. Trying to get five people together in a short amount of time would be difficult but I had to try.

After finagling back and forth in texts, we were able to get together the next evening. It was a Friday evening and everyone was available except for Alex, which turned out to be ok. Once the meeting was set, I began preparing what I wanted to say. I lay in bed Friday morning, praying and imagining what words the Holy Spirit would give me. Throughout the day, I asked our Blessed Mother to be right by my side when I told the kids. Even driving up to Ashley and Danny's, I was emotional just thinking about how the kids would receive this latest development. They had figured out something was up with the persistence I had shown in setting a time to get together and once we were all sitting in Ashley and Danny's living room, it didn't take long before Hailey said, "Ok, let's have it." Hailey has always been the one to cut to the chase.

I first told them that my tumor markers had gone down quite a bit, which was a great sign that the chemo was working and then went right into the heavy news. I was able to stay composed until I saw the sadness in my daughter's' eyes. It broke my heart. There were tears and at one point, Val said, "Why don't you give your girls a hug." From the first sign of tears, I wanted to hold them close to me but I also wanted to give them the space if they needed it. But, after Val's suggestion, I went to each one and held them tight, kissed them and told them how much I loved them.

I wanted them to feel free to ask anything that was on their mind, to share whatever was in their heart. The first thing that Sally said was that she felt selfish by saying she wanted me to be at her wedding but that it probably wouldn't happen. I wanted to take my baby girl onto my lap and comfort her, like I did when she was a little girl. Instead, I gently said that whether I would be physically present or not, I would still be there with her. It didn't make her feel any better at that moment but I thought that once we moved closer to that being a possibility, we would be able to share our thoughts of what her wedding may be like without me there, if that was God's will.

I told the kids that I had stopped by our parish office that day to see our pastor to let him know Val and I would like to meet with him and I picked up a packet to begin planning my funeral. Hailey asked why dad and I planned to meet with our parish priest so soon; was it because I thought my dying was coming sooner than I was letting on or was it that I just wanted to make plans for my funeral ahead of time. I assured her that I was just trying to get things in order and planned so that it would be less stress for the family, including myself, when things got more difficult at the end.

Finally, Val expressed how important it was to celebrate the time we had together, the holidays, the weddings, Hailey's soccer games, Sally's play…. And Ashley casually added, "a baby in May!" We all looked at Ashley in totally shock and the most joyous tears and exclamations came from our hearts as we all went to hug Ashley and Danny to congratulate them on becoming parents and praising God for his goodness!

It was a total shift of gears and I NEVER thought that was the way the evening was going to go! But, God had the perfect plan, AGAIN!

> "I will show you what someone is like who comes to me, hears my words, and acts on them. That one is like a man building a house, who dug deeply and laid the foundation on rock; when a flood arose, the river burst against that house but could not shake it, because it had been well built." (Luke 6:47-48)

A few days later, I received a letter from Hailey that she wrote to me the day after we all got together. Reflecting on the gospel from Luke she had just read, here is part of her letter:

> I think that's our family. I really believe that we are blessed to know and be aware that the flood is coming. I think of my friends and my teammates….if their parent died, they would be caught

totally off guard. But we have had the opportunity to prepare. Because our family places our trust in the Lord and <u>relies on Jesus for our strength,</u> when the flood comes, we won't be shaken. And knowing that, we can put our minds and hearts at rest so we can enjoy each moment together! We have such an incredible family! Thank you, Lord! I love you, mom!

The Joy of the Lord is my strength.

NEHEMIAH 8:10

Shifting Gears

FOR MOST OF THE PAST SEVERAL YEARS, my health has been the focus of our family. Yes, there was Val's cancer that I shared with you and my mom's cancer, but there were also other members of our family that have gone through health issues that I haven't shared. We have been very blessed with healthy daughters and besides ACL surgery on my daughter, Hailey's knee due to a tear while playing soccer at University of St. Thomas, we continue to be blessed. However, while playing in a couple of games, Hailey's heart began racing faster than normal. She wasn't sure what was going on but soon, her heart rate slowed down and she dismissed the symptoms she had. But, in one game, her heart rate did not slow down, even after being taken out of the game and 30 minutes after that. We knew she needed to be taken to the ER to be checked out because heart issues are very serious.

She had labs drawn, an ultrasound done on her heart, an EKG, an echocardiogram and finally an MRI to find out what caused her rapid heart rate. After spending a few days in the hospital and many roller coaster rides, the doctors agreed that she could participate in soccer again. The increased heart rate could have possibly been an isolated incident so Hailey will continue to be aware of what her body is telling her and will seek care if she needs it.

Our family had shifted gears from caring for me to caring for Hailey during that scary time. As I processed and prayed about what was going on with Hailey, I found myself being very emotional and I tried to identify what emotions I was feeling. Just a week prior, Hailey called to share her great news of getting engaged to Alex and after that phone call, I could not stop crying. Of course, I was overjoyed with the news, just as I was when our oldest daughter, Ashley, called to announce her engagement to Danny, but there seemed to be something more than joy that was making me so emotional.

It wasn't until the next morning, when I woke up and lay in bed thanking God for another day and remembering that Hailey and Alex were engaged that the word, "relieved" came to my heart, along with more tears. Relieved? Yes. Relieved that the probability of being present for Hailey and Alex's wedding was greater since it was actually going to happen. We believed that Hailey and Alex would get married; it was just a matter of when he would propose. With my future being more unpredictable than most, (remember, everyone's future is unpredictable) the wonder of whether I would be here for anything in the future was always on my mind and in my heart.

The gospel reading for the Sunday that Hailey was in the hospital waiting for answers was from Matthew about a wedding banquet and who would be prepared for it, it was very providential for our situation.

> Once more Jesus spoke to them in parables, saying: "The kingdom of heaven may be compared to a king who gave a wedding banquet for his son. He sent his slaves to call those who had been invited to the wedding banquet, but they would not come. Again he sent other slaves, saying, 'Tell those who have been invited: Look, I have prepared my dinner, my oxen and my fat calves have been slaughtered, and everything is ready; come to the wedding banquet.' But they made light of it and went away, one to his farm, another to his business, while the rest seized his slaves, mistreated them, and killed them. The king was enraged. He sent his troops, destroyed those murderers, and burned their city. Then he said to his slaves, 'The wedding is ready, but those invited were not worthy. Go therefore into the main streets, and invite everyone you find to the wedding banquet.' Those slaves went out into the streets and gathered all whom they found, both good and bad; so the wedding hall was filled with guests.
>
> "But when the king came in to see the guests, he noticed a man there who was not wearing a wedding robe, and he said to him, 'Friend, how did you get in here without a wedding robe?' And he was speechless. Then the king said to the attendants, 'Bind him hand and foot, and throw him into the outer darkness, where there will be weeping and gnashing of teeth.' For many are called, but few are chosen." (Matthew 22:1-14)

Are we accepting the invitation to the wedding banquet? After helping Ashley plan her wedding, and then Hailey, the guest list was probably the biggest and most difficult part of the planning. With our huge families, the number of guests was large and then to have to choose where to draw the line of who to invite was tough. But in the parable, Jesus tells us that everyone is invited to His heavenly banquet, we just need to accept the invitation. We need to be ready, wearing our best wedding garment. How do we do that? By preparing our heart to receive Jesus. Each time we attend mass, we are being invited to the banquet table of the Lord, by receiving the Eucharist. Each time we offer our day up for the glory of God, we are opening our hearts to receive Him in the Eucharist. Each time we see the face of Jesus in others, we are growing closer to Him and readies ourselves to share the Heavenly banquet with Him.

Be ready and keep ready, you and all the companies that are assembled around you, and hold yourselves in reserve for them.

EZEKIEL 38:7

Fill 'Er Up!

SITTING IN ADORATION, I wanted to just be still and let Jesus fill my heart. The chapel was very quiet with just the hum of the fan filling the space. My breathing slowed down with each breath as I relaxed in Jesus' love for me. I thanked Him for all He has given me and I asked Him what He would like me to do for Him. I sat quietly for about 40 minutes before I felt the need to journal my thoughts.

I was barely able to hold my pen to write because my fingers were so sensitive due to the beginning stages of neuropathy caused by the chemo I was taking. My handwriting was barely legible because I needed to hold my pen differently so I didn't feel the discomfort in my fingertips. I was wondering if it will continue to worsen and become irreversible at some point. My oncologist said that I could stop taking my chemo a few days earlier than when my off week started. Hopefully, that would help in it not being long lasting. But, if the neuropathy did continue, it would become more difficult to journal by writing, I would have to type my journals or dictate my thoughts.

As I looked at Christ on the cross, I realized that I was experiencing His five wounds: the neuropathy in my hands and feet and the cancer that is throughout my mid-section. I felt very close to Jesus at that moment. Although, my pain didn't even compare to what Jesus suffered, it helped me understand the love He has for me to die on the cross for me, and you! I thanked Him again for suffering for me and for dying for me.

Those are very special moments that encourage me and strengthen me, filling my spiritual gas tank, to continue to trust the journey that I am on and to appreciate every small grace that is given to me.

> Now as they went on their way, he entered a certain village, where a woman named Martha welcomed him into her home. She had a sister named Mary, who sat at the Lord's feet and listened to what he was saying. But Martha was distracted by her many tasks; so she came to him and asked, "Lord, do you not care that my sister has left me to do all the work by myself? Tell her then to help me." But the Lord answered her, "Martha, Martha, you are worried and distracted by many things; there is need of only one thing. Mary has chosen the better part, which will not be taken away from her." (Luke 10:38-42)

The story about Jesus' visit to the home of Mary and her sister Martha has a message for everyone. Although I have slowed down the pace of my life quite a bit in the past few years and especially in the last several months, I still find times when I'm living like Martha, when I really should be living like Mary.

On one hand, I see that Martha is doing her best to serve Jesus and that is what we have been called to do. But it was her attitude toward Mary that blinded her of the true sense of service. She was jealous that Mary was simply sitting at the feet of Jesus, listening to him.

I remember the first time I heard this reading about the two sisters. Coming from a large family, there were always chores to do. There were many times when I had to dust different rooms in the house. It was one of my least favorite chores to do because it was very time consuming and tedious. We had a set of bookshelves that had what seemed like a 100 nik naks on it! It didn't matter what anyone else had to do, I was jealous of my siblings because I felt they had barely anything to do compared to me!

That childhood feeling came rushing back to me when I read about how Martha felt that day. That feeling quickly dissipated, though, as I continued reading what Jesus told Martha.

"Martha, Martha, you are anxious and worried about many things. There is need of only one thing. Mary has chosen the better part and it will not be taken from her."

Although Mary had chosen to sit at Jesus' feet and learn from Him, her job wasn't as easy as it originally appeared. Jesus, most likely, told Mary and all who listened, what He wanted them to do to Glorify God. As we know, sharing our faith can be very difficult at times but if we listen and learn from Jesus, we will be given grace and courage to talk to others about our faith.

Now, if you would take a look at the dust building up in my own house (but, don't look too closely!), you can see that I 'let the house go' in order to spend time with Jesus and learn from Him how to better share my faith with others.

Are you a Martha or a Mary?

Martha: Are your Sunday's filled with athletic events and "Hail Mary" passes?

Mary: Are your Sunday's filled with family gatherings and a family rosary?

Martha: Do you drop your kids off at Faith Formation and run to get groceries before picking them up again?

Mary: Do you drop your kids off and stop in at the Adoration Chapel to spend time with Jesus so He can feed your soul?

Martha: Do you spend "free time" checking facebook, twitter, or other social media to see what everyone else is doing?

Mary:Do you find time to read quality books (you are what you read): and find out what Jesus is doing?

Believe me, I'm both Mary and Martha, but I am making an effort to be more like Mary each day. Won't you join me?

Look to the Lord and his strength;
seek his face always.

1 CHRONICLES 16:11

No End in Sight

THE MONTHS FOLLOWING my heart to heart talk with my doctor, I have had some highly emotional moments that may have challenged my faith if I didn't have such a deep relationship with Jesus and His mother. Some say that God tests our faith at times like these but I say that He is giving us opportunities to grow our faith.

My hands and feet have healed after a time of ugliness as the skin on my feet literally peeled off in bits and pieces as a result of my chemo being too strong. My feet were sensitive but they never got bad enough that I couldn't walk, and believe me when I say, "Thank you, God!" I took three weeks off from treatment in order for my feet to heal and they did so beautifully. My fingers and fingernails never really peeled but they changed in looks and texture. They were also sensitive to bumps, cuts, and cracking and finally, felt much better. After having the break from chemo, I wondered what my tumor markers would be. I also cut back my daily intake of oral chemo from six pills daily to four pills daily. I was very pleasantly surprised that my tumor markers, indeed, went down. I was physically feeling really well for the first time in many months, which obviously pleased me and also pleased my doctor.

For the next four months, my tumor markers continue to drop a few points and they actually dropped low enough to be considered in the 'normal' range. Each month, my doctor and I would do a little cheer of thanksgiving for good lab results. I was very open with my doctor about my faith and belief in God's hand in my health by thanking Him and giving Him praise. She agreed with me!

Finally, in the fourth month of my tumor markers dropping and within the normal range, I asked my doctor if we could "make a call" because something was definitely going on, or should I say, NOT going on! She said yes. Now, remember, we could not say words like, "remission" or "cancer free" but we could use words like, "inactive cancer cells" and "maintenance". The doctor's best deduction in my case was that the cancer cells were inactive at the moment and I would continue with the same dosage of chemo to, hopefully, maintain good lab results. A bonus was that I didn't need to return to see her for two months, rather than seeing her every month, which I had been doing for the past few years. It may sound like a small victory, but it was still a victory!

And Jesus said, "Suppose one of you has a friend, and you go to him at midnight and say to him, 'Friend, lend me three loaves of bread; for a friend of mine has arrived, and I have nothing to set before him.' And he answers from within, 'Do not bother me; the door has already been locked, and my children are with me in bed; I cannot get up and give you anything.' I tell you, even though he will not get up and give him anything because he is his friend, at least because of his persistence he will get up and give him whatever he needs.

"So I say to you, Ask, and it will be given you; search, and you will find; knock, and the door will be opened for you. For everyone who asks receives, and everyone who searches finds, and for everyone who knocks, the door will be opened. Is there anyone among you who, if your child asks for a fish, will give a snake instead of a fish? Or if the child asks for an egg, will give a scorpion? If you then, who are evil, know how to give good gifts to your children, how much more will the heavenly Father give the Holy Spirit to those who ask him!" (Luke 11:5-13)

I have so many people that have persevered in prayer for me and I know their prayers are being heard and answered. A friend of mine, who prays for me every day, told me that she prays that I will live until I'm 80 years old! How sweet is that? I personally don't ask for that much time in my prayers, but if she wants to, that's just fine with me.

I pray to live and enjoy today and every day that I am blessed with.

I pray to be able to celebrate the birth of our first grandbaby in a few months.

I pray to be able to celebrate Sally's confirmation and Hailey and Alex's graduation from University of St. Thomas, all on the same day, within the same week that Ashley is due to deliver her baby girl!

I pray to be able to witness Hailey and Alex commit themselves to each other in the sacrament of marriage, just two weeks after they graduate from college.

I pray to be able to celebrate 25 years of marriage with my one and only Valentine, two weeks after Hailey and Alex's wedding. Our anniversary also happens to be the same day that Sally was born and she will be ever so sweet 16!

Throw in my birthday, Mother's Day, the anniversary of my diagnosis (yes, I celebrate that date), Ashley's birthday and the baptism of my granddaughter; I have a lot of special events to want to celebrate. Who wouldn't want to celebrate such wonderful events as I have described? For these reasons, I persevere in prayer and I believe God will answer my prayers. In fact, He already has! Many times! He has given me more time to do His will. Feeling as fabulous as I do AND my numbers looking as fabulous as they are, He has given me new sight, again. I have gone from planning my funeral, anticipating the end of life here, to looking ahead to all of the amazing events that are in my future! So, for right now, there is no end in sight!

Devote yourselves to prayer,
being watchful and thankful.
COLOSSIANS 4:2

The End Is Only the Beginning

S O, HERE WE ARE. You have just traveled a very adventurous journey with me and with Jesus. And we are not finished yet. Only God knows when we will cross the finish line of life. Until then, will you continue to walk me?

Throughout the book, I have focused on Jesus and all that He has done for me and wants to do for you and now, I want to share with you my point of view of what His mother, Mary, may have felt walking with Jesus to the cross.

> *But she was greatly troubled at what was said and pondered what sort of greeting this might be. (Luke 1:29)*

> *He went down with them and came to Nazareth, and was obedient to them; and His mother kept all these things in her heart. (Luke 2:51)*

Mary didn't know what God had planned for her or her Son but she remained strong in her faith, saying yes, again and again, as she carried Jesus in her womb, presented Him in the Temple, watched Him grow into a man, and then followed Him to the cross, where she stood by Him until He took His last breath. Like, Mary, I do not know what God has planned for me or for my family either, but I will remain steadfast in my faith and I will offer my 'yes' to whatever God asks of me.

There are so many things that I keep in my heart and "ponder" and I would like to share some with you. I hold tight thoughts of dying, which I have quite often. They aren't scary or sad thoughts, they're just thoughts. I think of what life will be like without me in the house; the everyday routines that will need to be done by Val or Sally. Doing the laundry, making meals, cleaning the house- all things that we must do to keep a home running smoothly but don't give much thought to it or even dislike doing. Believe me; I have given thought to it. It is a blessing when I realize that there will be a day that I won't be here to do these menial tasks for my family and when I do, I thank God that I am still here to serve them and God, even when I'm cleaning the toilet!

What I don't think of often are events that will take place in the distant future. I believe that I will be here to celebrate the list of exciting events that I listed in the past chapters but I don't give much thought further out than a few months. It isn't that I don't think I won't be here for them, but I am able to remain in the present and appreciate each exciting moment as it comes.

I mentioned earlier in the book about the steps I have taken to plan my funeral. When I learned of the possibility of a perforation in my bowel and its serious outcome, it really sent me on a path to write my wishes down and begin to prepare my family for my death. The more prepared I can be for that day, the more peace I have and hopefully, the more peace my family will have, too. My family has been quite amazing throughout this entire journey and I know they have grown stronger in their faith because of it but they really do not like to talk much about my dying, so I keep my thoughts in my heart, like Mary did. I know they would listen to whatever I have to say, if I really needed them to do so, but I'm not there yet. I hope when that time comes, it will give them as much peace as it gives me.

Something else that I think of often is when I am with someone, especially if it's someone I don't see often, I cherish the time I spend with them because it may be the last time I see them. I tell them how much I appreciate them, just in case I don't have the opportunity again. I have even gone as far as telling them that it may be the last time I see them. Does that sound harsh to you? It shouldn't. I wish everyone would think that way. *Do not boast about tomorrow, for you do not know what a day may bring. (Proverbs 27:1)* Why shouldn't we tell others how much we love them or appreciate them each time we see them?

When I think of all of the roles I have played in my life, I am truly blessed. Daughter, sister, wife, mother, grandmother, friend, servant, speaker, writer, leader, follower, patient, caregiver, classmate, teacher, student, decorator, prayer warrior, athlete, coach, cheerleader…the list can go on and on and there still may something I haven't done yet that God has planned for me. I'm willing to say yes again because I know that His plan for me is perfect and I know that He will provide me with whatever I need to accomplish it.

I believe another role I have taken on is one that I can't quite put a label on but let me describe it for you. Because I have been given so much grace throughout my journey, I have been able to be open to share just about everything I have endured so that you can feel like you are not alone as you carry your cross. I talked about things that you have in your heart but may be afraid to talk about. And, I talked about dying. I want you to embrace, what everyone will eventually do, without fear or sadness. I want you to appreciate what you have been given and to understand that life on earth is just a moment in time. I want you to believe that there is a God who loves you and that eternal life in heaven is awaiting you. I want you to know the truth of God's love and receive the graces that He showers down upon you. I want everyone to have what I have! The joy! The peace! The love! With cancer or without! With whatever cross you are carrying.

I hope this book has inspired you create or deepen your relationship with Jesus, knowing that He has been walking with you on your journey of life and wants to give you whatever you need.

If I may, I would like to ask for your prayers for me and my family and please know that I will pray for you.

God Bless!

And Mary kept all these things,
reflecting on them in her heart.
LUKE 2:19